Enzo Bianchi was born in Castel Boglione, Piedmont, Italy, in 1943. In 1965, after graduating from the University of Turin, he founded an ecumenical monastic community – the Bose Community – of which he is still the prior. Fr Bianchi is a well-known author of books on *lectio divina* and the spiritual life, which have been translated into many languages. He has dedicated himself to the search for spirituality capable of giving life to Christians today and furthering communion among all people.

The Bose Community now numbers over 80 brothers and sisters of various Christian traditions, and receives thousands of visitors annually.

Also available by the author in this series published by SPCK: *Words of Spirituality* (2002, 2012).

GOD, WHERE ARE YOU?

Enzo Bianchi

Translated by Susan Leslie

Originally published in Italy in 2008
as *Dio, dove sei?* by Rizzoli
Copyright © RCS Libri 2008, 2011

First published in Great Britain in 2014

Society for Promoting Christian Knowledge
36 Causton Street
London SW1P 4ST
www.spckpublishing.co.uk

English translation copyright © SPCK 2014

Unless otherwise noted, Scripture quotations are taken from the New Revised Standard Version of
the Bible, Anglicized Edition, copyright © 1989, 1995 by the Division of Christian Education of the
National Council of the Churches of Christ in the USA. Used by permission. All rights reserved.
Extracts marked KJV are from the Authorized Version of the Bible (The King James Bible),
the rights in which are vested in the Crown, and are reproduced by permission of
the Crown's Patentee, Cambridge University Press.
Extracts marked NEB are from the New English Bible, copyright © The Delegates of the Oxford
University Press and The Syndics of Cambridge University Press, 1961, 1970. Used by permission.

British Library Cataloguing-in-Publication Data
A catalogue record for this book is available from the British Library

ISBN 978–0–281–06959–0
eBook ISBN 978–0–281–06960–6

Typeset by Graphicraft Limited, Hong Kong
First printed in Great Britain by Ashford Colour Press
Subsequently digitally printed in Great Britain

eBook by Graphicraft Limited, Hong Kong

Produced on paper from sustainable forests

One day, when he was receiving learned guests, Rabbi Mendel of Kozk astounded them by asking all of a sudden, 'Where does God dwell?' They laughed at him: 'What's the matter with you? Isn't the world full of his glory?' But the rabbi himself answered his question: 'God dwells where he is allowed to enter.'

(M. Buber, *The Way of Man*)

Contents

Series Foreword

To read Enzo Bianchi's work is, among other things, to be force-fully made aware that we have got used to a rather thin diet of resources to help us read the Bible. We have plenty of good scholar-ship and plenty of good popular summaries of that scholarship – but very little on the actual *theology* of reading the Bible, very little on reading the Bible as a central form of our *discipleship*. Twentieth-century theology has left us with a great heritage of recovering and reworking some of the major themes in the kind of scriptural study practised in the early or medieval Church or in the Reformation: Henri de Lubac, Karl Barth and others have helped us question the bland modern assumption that the Bible is primarily a set of historical texts, to be read and understood by criteria external to themselves. All but the narrowest of conserva-tive Protestant theology has moved some distance away from that other modern assumption which sees Scripture as a guaranteed source of unquestionably reliable information and little more. But how then should we understand the relationship between our common life and prayer and our study of Scripture?

Fr Enzo often returns in one way or another to the theme of 'epiclesis' – the invocation of the Holy Spirit – as a focal act of the community, especially the monastic community. It is part of the way in which we live as Christians with a keen awareness of the age to come, the way we live eschatologically. And what the Holy Spirit does is to bring us face to face with the Word of God, the living action of the Second Person of the Trinity. Thus if we read Scripture as we must, invoking the Holy Spirit, what we encounter in Scripture is that living Word. We are made contemporary with what Scripture witnesses to; we discover the *unity* of Scripture not in any theory but in the person of Jesus Christ, on whom the whole of Scripture converges and around whom it finds its shape.

For Fr Enzo, this is the key to an extraordinarily broad range of reflection – on priesthood, on religious life, on the challenges of contemporary European society, on the daily struggle and frustration of being a Christian. If it is true that there is no way of finding or being found by God that is not also a finding of one's own humanity, then what is happening in the scriptural encounter is an unveiling of who we are – as human beings and as the particular people we happen to be. In this encounter we meet the God who has already become present in us and seeks to be made known through us; we become a place where God's glory can be manifest. The variety of scriptural narrative is testimony to the diversity of the modes of God's presence in each one. So as we read, in community, in company with our brothers and sisters, we are doubly alert – to what we are being taught about the calling, dignity and destiny of men and women, and to what we are learning about our own calling and gifting.

The reading of Scripture is a genuinely sacramental event, one in which God's act in the past, the present and the future is laid bare to us and in which we are ourselves caught up in that act. As we absorb the communication of the Word, we become contemporary with the events of primal revelation, and contemporary with the climax of history in which Christ is all in all. And it is in this way alone that we become truly contemporary with our own times. We may think there is no problem about being 'contemporary' here and now; but the truth is that, without an anchorage in the Word of God, we are insubstantial, distracted by our own private agendas and incapable of truthful relationship with each other. Our communion with God the Word, realized in our communion as readers together of the written vehicle of the Word, delivers us from this shadow world and equips us to give voice to something of God's perspective on the world we inhabit – both as celebrants of the environment in which we stand and as hopeful critics of a human world that is profoundly confused and conflicted.

Fr Enzo's books are a powerful witness to what the monastic calling can still make possible in our time. Behind all he writes stands the practice of the community at Bose, a community that has offered a unique remodelling of the traditions of classical monasticism in a style that is compelling for countless people today. It is a community in which the corporate study of Scripture is central; those who have experienced biblical reflection in community at Bose will know what an extraordinary experience it is, an opening of unimagined depths in the text. But the friends and guests of Bose will also recognize how this approach shapes the whole ethos of worship through a liturgy that, like all the best monastic liturgies, lays out the wholeness of scriptural imagery and narrative in all its rich interconnection and interdependence. Fr Enzo's writing shows how this, far from creating an inward-looking, 'aesthetic' spirit, provides the resources we need as Christians to bring real illumination to the confusions of our culture.

Enzo Bianchi is one of the most significant Christian voices in Europe. He shows what can be achieved by an immersion in Scripture that involves both intellect and imagination alike, and – in common with all the most serious Christian voices of our day – he cannot be labelled as a partisan 'liberal' or 'traditionalist'. He offers exactly what the monastic voice at its truest has always offered: a way into the heart of our ecclesial and social questions that is honest, patient and sensitive. His is a perspective that the English-speaking Christian world should welcome enthusiastically.

Rowan Williams
Magdalene College, Cambridge

Introduction

All our life, we hear in the depths of our heart a gentle whisper, like a still small voice (cf. 1 Kings 19.12, KJV): 'Where are you?' This is the first word that God addresses to human beings who have discovered that they are capable of self-determination, able to choose and to do evil (cf. Gen. 3.9). 'Where are you?' that is: what stage have you reached in the process of becoming human, a work of art to be created with intelligence, love and freedom? This is the real question, the decisive one for every man and woman under the sun. Only by answering this question do we realize who we are, what we are becoming, our responsibility to others and to the world. To answer this question means to 'search for man', *quaerere hominem*, a task that cannot be shirked either by those who believe in God or those who do not.

However, there are times in our lives when, perhaps prompted by this fundamental question that God poses through our conscience, we are led to ask another question: 'God, where are you?' We address this question to God: either we have faith in him and he is the object of our desire and our quest, or we question him with suspicion and mistrust. 'God, where are you?' is a question that sometimes springs from anguish in times of suffering, solitude or despair; at other times it arises from a loving, nostalgic desire for him whom we love but who remains invisible to us.

Every day, we have to overcome doubt, begin to believe again and renew our faith, thanks to the love we feel within ourselves for the Lord. Yes, love overcomes our doubts, our lack of faith, our incredulity. This way is not madness, it does not set aside or offend reason, but it is the breath of life: faith leads to love and love to faith.

The following pages, resulting from my close study of the Bible, seek only to echo stories of encounters between God and human beings, between God and those whom he chose, called and loved because they had sought God, prompted, dare one say, by God himself. The stories are varied because God is met in various ways. They are encounters in which God shows himself unexpectedly, not as we are used to thinking of him: he is a God who surprises us, astonishes us, contradicts us and at times even seems to be against us. These biblical passages are sometimes dramatic, like a struggle between adversaries, and sometimes full of joy, like the union of marriage.

As we read these stories, we learn what Christianity is: we come to know a God who came to us in human form, who came among us by making himself one of us. Jesus of Nazareth is the image of the invisible God (cf. John 1.18; Col. 1.15); he is his face: a God made human, a man in whom the living God has lived and continues to live.

'God, where are you?' we cry.

'Where are *you*?' cries God.

In this dialogue of cries and questions lies our true identity: we are human beings called to become God.

1

The faith of Abraham

Rabbi Judah said: 'The whole world was going in one direction and Abraham was going in the other.'

(*Genesis Rabbah* 42.8)

Abraham . . . is the father of all of us, as it is written: 'I have made you the father of many nations' [Gen. 17.5] . . . in the presence of the God in whom he believed, who gives life to the dead and calls into existence the things that do not exist.

(Rom. 4.16–17)

Abraham had not received anything from God, yet he believed in the one who promised; that is the faith that is truly worthy of praise and renown.   (Augustine, *Sermons* 113A.10)

Introduction

According to the Bible, the first human being who encountered the true and living God, heard his word and obeyed it, is Abraham. His story is told in the book of Genesis, chapters 12 to 25.[1] Abraham is the great father of the people of Israel, and indeed generations of Jews will call him *abinu*, 'our father'. This denotes father in the religious as well as the genealogical sense: father in the faith, so much so that God will be defined as 'the God of Abraham'.

What is certain is that various traditions have come together in the pages that tell Abraham's story. These were at first transmitted orally, then reread and edited and eventually given their final form in the book of Genesis at the time of the Jewish exile in Babylon in the sixth century BC. What, in short, does Abraham's story and its position in the first book of the Bible tell us? It tells us that God wanted the world and the human race to be free; moved by his ecstatic love, God created, by his Word and his Spirit, everything that exists. In the creation stories (Gen. 1—2), the origins and the *telos*, the purpose, of the world and of humankind are revealed. From creation onwards, the manifestations of man's sin and failure emerge, real wounds inflicted on God's creative purpose. Adam and Eve do not accept their condition of creatures (Gen. 3); Cain kills his brother Abel (Gen. 4); mankind grows in violence and malice to the point of causing the flood (Gen. 6—7); the tower of Babel is built in the name of totalitarian political and cultural power (Gen. 11.1–9). The man and woman created by God, called to a task that should have borne fruit in a full life and in justice and peace, show their capacity for evil, demonstrating that the way they have taken is one that leads to death and so needs salvation.

In that prehistory of mankind, which has some of the features of myth, evil grows and increases rapidly. But in that same history, although death and destruction are possible, human beings bear 'the image and likeness of God' (cf. Gen. 1.26) imprinted on them by God at creation, and they 'search for God and perhaps grope for him' (Acts 17.27). Abel offers sacrifices pleasing to God (Gen. 4.4); Enoch's generation 'began to invoke the name of the LORD' (Gen. 4.26); Enoch 'walked with God' (Gen. 5.24); Noah 'found favour in the sight of the LORD' (Gen. 6.8), so much so that, after the flood, the Lord himself renews through him his blessing on all creation and establishes a covenant, a pact of life, with every living being (Gen. 9.8–17).

The God who in the beginning created the world with his word (Gen. 1.3, 6ff.) wants to begin history anew with his same word. He wants to start the history of salvation, in which he decides to make himself known and reveal himself to his creatures. This history begins precisely with Abraham, whom God calls, chooses and separates from other people, the children of Adam who have embarked on ways of death. It is through Abraham that God will offer mankind a way to return to him. If Adam is the figure of totality, of unity (*omnis homo Adam*), Abraham is the figure of difference. He is a man, he belongs to mankind, he is at one with human history but at the same time he is called to be different. He is chosen and separated to make a journey that will bring everyone to God, carrying God's blessing, that is, life and peace, to all peoples.

Man, created by God in his image and likeness, is *capax Dei*, capable of knowing God, of being in relationship with God, even in the darkness of evil, and Abraham is the man to whom God turns, making himself known and meeting him. According to the Bible, Abraham does not emerge from absolute darkness but from a humanity that in its sin and ignorance had sought God in many religious ways, which were, however, tainted by idolatry. What is specific to Abraham, then, is his faith, his adherence to God who called him personally, a faith that shows itself first of all as a break with the idolatry of his fathers. Several centuries later, Joshua will see Abraham's story in this light:

> Thus says the LORD, the God of Israel: Long ago your ancestors – Terah and his sons Abraham and Nahor – lived beyond the Euphrates and served other gods. Then I took your father Abraham from beyond the River and led him through all the land of Canaan. (Josh. 24.2–3)

Indeed, in the background of Abraham's story is the dispersion of the peoples that took place after Babel, but God, in his faithful love for man, desires to transform this process of dispersion and corruption into a way of communion and fullness of life. To this end, he calls Abraham, and this calling forth leads finally to communion. Abraham will be the father not only of the people of Israel but of all who believe in the true and living God.

'Go . . . to the land that I will show you'

In the Bible, Abraham's name appears for the first time in the genealogy of the flood, a genealogy that bears witness to the increase of mankind blessed by God through his covenant with

Noah. Among the descendants of Shem, Noah's son, it is written that Terah was 70 years old when he begot Abraham, Nahor and Haran (Gen. 11.26). At this point, however, the chain of generations appears to be interrupted because Abraham's wife Sarai is sterile, and so cannot give him offspring (Gen. 11.30). In a caravan led by his father, Abraham leaves Ur of the Chaldeans in lower Mesopotamia and migrates to the land of Canaan, crossing the territory of Haran on the way. At Haran, however, Abraham's father Terah dies (Gen. 11.32) and so the goal is not reached.

It is just after his father's death in the land of Haran that God calls Abraham. Thus the first encounter between Abraham and the living God takes place, not in the form of a vision but in that of a word. It is a sudden, unexpected encounter and the reader of Genesis recognizes in chapter 12 a true new beginning: the start of the history of salvation. 'The LORD said to Abram, "Go [*lekh lekha*] from your country and your kindred and your father's house to the land that I will show you"' (Gen. 12.1). One word from God resounds in Abram's heart. It is short, simple and disconcertingly sober, and at the same time it is new; it has never been heard before. It is a word that surprises Abram and shows that it was not he who had chosen to encounter God but God in his freedom and love who had wanted to encounter him. It is a word addressed directly to Abram, saying 'you' as when two human beings meet, yet it is God's word to man, God's first word to man in history, according to Scripture.

This word begins with an invitation: *Lekh lekha*, an expression which literally means 'go towards yourself'. It is an invitation to leave on a journey that is also interior, comparable in some way to the famous *gnôthi sautón*, 'know yourself', of traditional Greek wisdom. Abram continues his father Terah's migration but he is called to enter more deeply into the strange environment in which he finds himself, to travel further and in a sense towards a new destination. In obeying the command to 'Go!', he has first of all to make a break with three things:

- with the land from which he has come;
- with his idolatrous religious environment;[2]
- with his father's house, that is, with his kinship ties.[3]

The Lord's call is gratuitous, sovereign and free; it is motivated by love for humanity but it also represents a challenge because it asks for separations that are ever more deep and demanding. God asks us to 'leave for', to 'go from . . . in order to move towards'.[4] It is necessary to take leave of what is known and gives security, and go towards something new that involves risk: for a new life, a true life of communion, it is absolutely essential to free oneself from old ties, because 'without a clean break, a good communion is not possible' (Salomon Resnik). Yet how hard it is to understand this fact and what a temptation it is to go straight ahead, dragging the heavy burden of what lies behind, the past.

Here we can ask ourselves why exactly God chose Abram. The biblical texts give us no answer: it is not said that Abram was better than other men or that he was righteous and pleasing to God, as it was said of Noah. No, the call of God is due to nothing but his ecstatic love, which needs to go out of itself into someone else, a 'beloved': this call is not a response to the merits or virtues of the one called, nor is it a matter of destiny or predestination: no, the reason belongs to the mystery of God!

However, the most vital thing for us is that, in that personal call to Abram, the love of God for all human beings is revealed. For Abram, that call cannot be a privilege or a reward but only an assumption of responsibility in favour of all. Always the call of God first distinguishes, elects and separates from others, then shows itself as a call in favour of others. Election and universality are not contradictory but closely related: universality prevents election from becoming a privilege and, conversely, election prevents universality from disappearing into an anonymity that recognizes no personal responsibility. So, for Abram, his vocation means first of all believing in the word of God addressed to him, obeying that word truly, concretely and promptly, and then growing in hope on behalf of others.

After the command 'Go' comes the destination: 'to the land that I will show you'. God does not specify where and does not give a name to the promised land but asks Abram to have faith, to believe in the words 'I will show you'. First faith, then the indication of the goal: man must arise and walk in complete obedience, then, when he is already on the way, God will make clear the goal.

'In you all the families of the earth shall be blessed'

The call is followed by the promise addressed by the Lord to Abram:

> I will make of you a great nation, and I will bless you, and make your name great, so that you will be a blessing. I will bless those who bless you, and the one who curses you I will curse; and in you all the families of the earth shall be blessed.
>
> (Gen. 12.2–3)

The blessing, that is, the power of salvation and fullness of life, comes down from God and spreads through Abram to all humankind. Abram is the one chosen and blessed by God so that, in the course of history, the blessing may reach all human beings. God loves everyone and desires that all may be saved; he desires to communicate this will of his to all mankind through one man, Abram.

Yet there are contradictions and paradoxes in this divine will to bless, because it takes shape through the thoughts, words and deeds of men among themselves and before God. Abram is the 'son' of Terah, the 'husband' of Sarai and the 'uncle' of Lot, but he is not and cannot be 'father' on account of his wife's sterility. For the culture of those times, the first and most important fruit of God's blessing on a man was fatherhood, his fecundity in begetting children (cf. Gen. 1.28; 9.1, 7). God, then, blesses Abram, yet Abram's condition seems to impede the blessing: how can he, who cannot have a child, be the 'father of many nations' (Rom. 4.17)? Abram, however, has faith and obeys the Lord's command without hesitation. 'So Abram went, as the LORD had told him; and Lot went with him. Abram was seventy-five years old when he departed from Haran' (Gen. 12.4). So Abram goes forth towards a future, the only guarantee of which is the Lord's call. This is his faith, his adherence to the Lord with unfaltering trust, remaining firm without being shaken, looking to the Lord rather than to himself or his own thoughts, calculations or reasons. This is the attitude of faith, never assumed once and for all but renewed every day because man is constantly tempted, put to the test and contradicted by the vicissitudes of life.

Once he has reached the land of Canaan, Abram does not stop in any one place but leads the life of a shepherd, a pilgrim in search of fresh pastures. He will not pitch his tent in one place but will have to pitch it and take it down more than once, at Shechem, then to the east of Bethel, then in the Negev (cf. Gen. 12.5–9).

God promised Abram that he would make him see a land, but in reality it is God himself who makes himself 'seen' by Abram, saying that he will not give the land to him but to his offspring (Gen. 12.7). At times the new things that happen appear to be a denial of the words previously spoken by God.

Thus Abram must keep in his heart the promise of the 'land that God will make him see', but he will learn not to possess any land, to remain a stranger and pilgrim, a foreigner in the midst of another people. He has to learn that on earth there are no goals attained once and for all, no definitive points of arrival. God leaves man restless and asks him to go further, 'from beginning to beginning towards beginnings that have no end',[5] and the fulfilment of his promise, which is not a fulfilment of human desires, will come only in the kingdom.

With great spiritual understanding and with an audacity that even seems to contradict many pages of the Old Testament, the author of the Letter to the Hebrews writes:

> By faith Abraham obeyed when he was called to set out for a place that he was to receive as an inheritance; and he set out,

not knowing where he was going . . . For he looked forward
to the city that has foundations, whose architect and builder
is God . . . All of these [Abram and the other patriarchs] died
in faith without having received the promises, but from a
distance they saw and greeted them. They confessed that they
were strangers and foreigners on the earth, for people who
speak in this way make it clear that they are seeking a home-
land. If they had been thinking of the land that they had left
behind, they would have had opportunity to return. But as
it is, they desire a better country, that is, a heavenly one.
Therefore God is not ashamed to be called their God; indeed,
he has prepared a city for them.   (Heb. 11.8, 10, 13–16)

Abram received from God the promise of a land, but God accus-
tomed him in this way to await another city, prepared for all
humankind, a city that is God himself, as Ezekiel understood: 'And
the name of the city from that time on shall be, The LORD is There'
(Ezek. 48.35).

Abram believed God, and it was reckoned to him as righteousness

Abram, the father of Israel's faith and the faith of all believers,
by faith 'obeyed, set out, stayed' (cf. Heb. 11.8–9). But his faith
was more than once shaken and tempted. Abram believed with
great difficulty but unfailingly, 'hoping against hope' (Rom. 4.18),
without despair. It is for this firm faith that he was judged by God
to be a faithful believer and credited by God with righteousness.

In the years following his call, Abram with his family and flocks
wanders over the land of Canaan from north to south. In a period
of famine, he goes down to Egypt (Gen. 12.10–20); he has an argu-
ment with his nephew Lot and finally separates from him (Gen.
13); he is involved in the first armed conflict between opposing
kingdoms and in that situation carries out an act of liberation
(Gen. 14.1–16). Then he meets the mysterious Melchizedek,[6] king

of Salem and the first priest mentioned in the Bible, a pagan priest of *El Elyon*, the most high God (Gen. 14.17–20). This meeting is marked by the sign of blessing that begins to spread among the peoples; the pagan religions begin to feel an attraction towards the God of Abram. Thus Abram is blessed with an offering of bread and wine and pays a tithe to Melchizedek: an exchange of gifts, reciprocal recognition, a blessing that is passed on to others.

But the years pass and God's promise to Abram of numerous offspring does not seem to be fulfilled. Here, then, comes the night of faith for Abram. He had responded promptly to his calling and lived in hope for all those years afterwards, but now he sees himself and his wife Sarai growing old, while the promise remains unfulfilled. Abram had always listened to the Lord but now he dares to speak boldly, setting before him all his pain and bitter disillusionment.

> O Lord God, what will you give me, for I continue childless, and the heir of my house is Eliezer of Damascus? . . . You have given me no offspring, and so a slave born in my house is to be my heir. (Gen. 15.2–3)

It is Abram's night, in which the word of God seems to have been spoken in vain. This time, however, he meets God not only in words but also in a vision, a synthesis that involved his 'spiritual senses'.[7] In that dead-end situation, Abram suggests to God the possibility of solving the problem of offspring in a human way. Grown old by now, he will resort to adopting his servant Eliezer to guarantee posterity for himself.

The Lord, however, repeats to him firmly: 'This man shall not be your heir; no one but your very own issue shall be your heir' (Gen. 15.4). Then God has Abram come outside and invites him to look at the heavens, saying to him, 'Look towards heaven and count the stars, if you are able to count them . . . So shall your descendants be' (Gen. 15.5). God asks Abram to fix his gaze on an invisible beyond, starting from the stars in the sky, and Abram renews his faith. 'And he believed the Lord; and the Lord reckoned it to him as righteousness' (Gen. 15.6). This brief verse, quoted three times in the New Testament (Rom. 4.3; Gal. 3.6; Jas. 2.23), is a synthesis of the reality of faith in God, a faith capable of making a person righteous (cf. Hab. 2.4), not an intellectual process but an attitude that involves the whole self. To encounter God and to enter into relationship with him, it is necessary to have the faith and confidence expressed by the verbal roots *aman*, used in this passage, which means 'attachment, adhesion, tie', and *batak*, which means 'to trust, have confidence, stand on solid ground'. This is what faith is: placing one's confidence in God alone, receiving from him firmness and stability (cf. Isa. 7.9). This makes Abram 'the friend of God' (Jas. 2.23).

However, in this new encounter of God with Abram, something strange happens. It is not only night in Abram's heart, but night has also fallen around him. In obedience to the Lord's command to celebrate a covenant rite (Gen. 15.8–10), he has prepared animals as victims, each divided in two, with the two halves facing each other. Now torpor, a profound sleep (*tarmedah*), falls on Abram and a shadowy terror, a terrible obscurity (*ema chashekha*), takes hold of him (Gen. 15.12). It is a night of fear, a night of obscurity, in which Abram seems to lose control of his own rationality, the believer seems to lose every connection to God and falls into terrible confusion. It is a night full of menace, in which the catastrophe of emptiness and absence of meaning seems to prevail. Abram had to move beyond his own narrow horizon (God 'brought him outside'), stop looking at himself (he invited him to 'look towards heaven') and go towards obscurity. It is a terrible test: it is not God who hides himself, becomes silent or evades the believer, but it is the believer who fails to listen to God, preferring to listen to the *tohu wa-bohu* (Gen. 1.2), the 'formless void' that dwells within.

In this terrifying darkness, however, come the words with which the Lord describes what awaits Abram's offspring: slavery in Egypt, oppression, exile, misfortune and the threat of destruction (Gen. 15.13–16). Thus Abram is called upon to recognize how relative are his own difficulties and tribulations, how slight in comparison to what will be the lot of his offspring. It is precisely when Abram has come out of himself in this way that God makes his covenant with him. In the darkness of night, fire and smoke pass between the divided animal victims ready for the sacrifice (Gen. 15.17). God makes himself present both in the brightness and in the dark. His presence burns like fire and is as fleeting and elusive as smoke; it is a presence that is seen and unseen, unveiled and immediately hidden. This elusive dialectic, this revelation and hiddenness of the Lord, is a sign of God's unconditional, universal and absolutely gratuitous covenant. 'On that day the LORD made a covenant with Abram, saying, 'To your descendants I give this land, from the river of Egypt to the great river, the river Euphrates' (Gen. 15.18). Abram receives the covenant but hears it repeated once more that the promise of land is for his offspring, not for him; the promise is always deferred, so as to be always renewed. This Abram learns in his night of fire.

'No longer shall your name be Abram, but your name shall be Abraham'

The years pass and Abram remains childless. Then his wife Sarai takes the initiative in an attempt to resolve the problem in a human way. She advises Abram to have sexual intercourse with their slave Hagar, who becomes pregnant and gives birth to Ishmael (Gen. 16.1–4, 15–16). This, however, leads to conflict in Abram's household (Gen. 16.4–14; 21.8–21). God's ways are not our ways.

When Abram was 99 years old, the Lord appeared to him and said, 'I am God Almighty; walk before me, and be blameless' (Gen. 17.1). Again there is a call to go out, to walk with integrity in God's presence; again there is the promise of a covenant. 'I will make my covenant between me and you, and will make you exceedingly numerous' (Gen. 17.2).

Then Abram fell on his face; and God said to him, 'As for me, this is my covenant with you: You shall be the ancestor of a

11

multitude of nations. No longer shall your name be Abram, but your name shall be Abraham; for I have made you the ancestor of a multitude of nations. I will make you exceedingly fruitful; and I will make nations of you, and kings shall come from you. I will establish my covenant between me and you, and your offspring after you throughout their generations, for an everlasting covenant, to be God to you and to your offspring after you.   (Gen. 17.3–7)

This time the covenant works both ways; it demands reciprocal faithfulness and takes effect through the efficacious sign of circumcision of the male genital organ (Gen. 17.9–14, 23–27). It is a sign of belonging to the Lord indelibly inscribed in the flesh, an act that entails the shedding of blood, that is, the offering of one's life to God. The covenant is sealed by the change of names from Abram to Abraham and Sarai to Sarah (Gen. 17.15). The Lord makes the elderly couple into a new creation. He gives them a new beginning, a new history for them and all humankind, always under the blessing of God. 'I will bless [Sarah], and moreover I will give you a son by her . . . and she shall give rise to nations; kings of peoples shall come from her' (Gen. 17.16). The rabbinic tradition wisely comments: 'Abram will not procreate, but Abraham will procreate; Sarai will not procreate, but Sarah will procreate' (*Genesis Rabbah* 44.10).

The story of Abram the believer becomes that of Abraham, the father of believers. This perspective, nevertheless, goes hand in hand with a faith that is not easy; even Abraham's faith is always tempted to waver in the face of human limitations. Abraham laughs bitterly, thinking that his age and that of his wife make the birth of a son impossible. 'O that Ishmael might live in your sight!' (Gen. 17.18). God grants this request but firmly repeats the promise and gives further details:

Your wife Sarah shall bear you a son, and you shall name him Isaac. I will establish my covenant with him as an everlasting covenant for his offspring after him . . . My covenant I will

establish with Isaac, whom Sarah shall bear to you at this
season next year.   (Gen. 17.19, 21)

And Abraham obeys, in a silence that bears witness to his definitive acceptance of God's word.

Conclusion

'I will give to you, and to your offspring after you, the land where
you are now an alien, all the land of Canaan, for a perpetual holding;
and I will be their God' (Gen. 17.8). These are the words addressed
by God to Abraham at the heart of the covenant. Yet, if we go to
the end of Abraham's story, we see that in reality he was always
'a stranger and an alien' (Gen. 23.4) in the land of Canaan. He
will die possessing only a small piece of ground acquired from
the Hittites, in which he will place a tomb for his wife Sarah and
for himself (Gen. 23; 25.7–11).

Abraham will never succeed in possessing the land, but his
greatness and his 'difference' lie in his capacity to adhere with full
confidence to God. It is his faith, persevering amid so many ordeals,
that has made him the 'father of believers' (cf. Rom. 4.16–17). In
fact, Abraham is always ready to begin anew from the beginning,
to start out on a journey *hic et nunc*, without letting himself be
trapped in the past or blinded by the future, which is, nevertheless,
full of promise. Faithful to the present moment, he reaches out

> towards a land that is not a land, towards a place that is not
> a place. The true 'Place', as the rabbinic tradition teaches
> us, is God . . . and the journey towards this 'Place' is an end-
> less adventure.[8]

2

Abraham and the binding of Isaac

God makes his voice heard in order to test your faith and put it to the proof. And you, Abraham, how do you react? What do you think? Perhaps you ponder in your heart: if the promise has been made to me and Isaac, and I now offer him in sacrifice, does it follow that I will not have to hope in that promise any more? Or do you rather think that he who made you the promise cannot lie and that, whatever may happen, the promise will remain valid?

(Origen, *Homilies on Genesis* 8.1)

> When they had surrendered, and he flung him
> upon his brow,
> We called unto him, 'Abraham,
> thou hast confirmed the vision . . .
> This is indeed the manifest trial.'
> And We ransomed him with a mighty sacrifice,
> and left for him among the later folk
> 'Peace be upon Abraham!'

(Qur'an 37.103–9)

The audacity of the story lies in attributing to God the demand for child sacrifice. It is as if God had said: 'You have given this impression of my cruelty, but I have come to assume it, because there is no other way of freeing you from it.'

(Paul Beauchamp, *Fifty Biblical Portraits*)

Introduction

After the birth of the son given to him by God, Abraham, by now 100 years old, circumcises the eight-day-old Isaac in obedience to the covenant (Gen. 21.4–5).

> The child grew, and was weaned; and Abraham made a great feast on the day that Isaac was weaned. But Sarah saw the son of Hagar the Egyptian, whom she had borne to Abraham, playing with her son Isaac. So she said to Abraham, 'Cast out this slave woman with her son; for the son of this slave woman shall not inherit along with my son Isaac.'
>
> (Gen. 21.8–10)

With a heavy heart, Abraham carries out his wife's wish and so Hagar and Ishmael are sent into the desert, where first they lose their way and risk dying of thirst, then, thanks to God's intervention, they regain their strength and beget a new clan with a new history (cf. Gen. 21.11–21). Thus Abraham has lost Ishmael, the son born of his slave; only the other son, Isaac, remains, to whom he is united by deep bonds of love. Isaac is the long-awaited son – exactly 25 years have passed since Abraham left Canaan (Gen. 12.4) – he is the son of God's promise, a promise whose fulfilment was deferred again and again (cf. Gen. 15.2–5; 17.15–21; 18.9–15). The progeny that God had promised to Abraham in the land for which he set out depends exclusively on this son.

This is the context of chapter 22 of Genesis, which Christian tradition calls the chapter of 'the sacrifice of Isaac'. Hebrew tradition, taking its cue from verse 9: 'Abraham . . . bound [verb 'aqad] his son Isaac', calls it instead the chapter of the 'binding of Isaac'. I, too, follow this tradition, in conformity with the letter of the biblical text, according to which Isaac was bound in preparation for sacrifice but was not actually sacrificed. The narrative opens with a kind of title, an enigmatic synthesis of the entire passage: 'After these things God tested Abraham' (Gen. 22.1), a verse that keeps us in suspense until the angel affirms: 'Now I know that you fear God' (Gen. 22.12). Between these two ends of the story, there unfolds a narrative that is awkward and difficult, perhaps even scandalous and certainly not easy to understand. This is a passage that first of all needs to be understood and commented on literally. Only then will it be possible to discuss some of the interpretations of Genesis 22; the more one reads and explains this text, the more questions it raises and the more disconcerting it appears.

Literal commentary

God's command

In the period since the first encounter with God (Gen. 12.1–3), Abraham has deepened his own faith and learned to abandon himself totally to the one who always carries out his promises. He is now a mature believer; he has reached old age, carrying out in total obedience the mandate God had given him. And now, with Isaac an adult, it is time for Abraham to acquire a fresh knowledge of God. After the call and promise sealed by the covenant, after the confirmation and fulfilment of that promise in Isaac's birth, now the moment of ultimate test arrives.

> God tested Abraham. He said to him, 'Abraham, Abraham!' And he said, 'Here I am.' He said, 'Take your son, your only son Isaac, whom you love, and go [*lekh lekha*] to the land of Moriah, and offer him there as a burnt-offering on one of the mountains that I shall show you.' (Gen. 22.1–2, adapted)

Why does God put Abraham to the test? One part of the rabbinic tradition answers that this test is the work of Satan; he persuades God to act in this way to see whether Abraham will remain faithful to him even in this situation, not simply in the good fortune that he had known up to that moment.[1] No more convincing than this naive explanation is that of some of the Church fathers, according to whom God intended to enhance Abraham's fame in the eyes of future ages.[2] The enigma remains and requires a more profound reading if we are to grasp it as a mystery that belongs to the realm of faith.

As at the beginning of Abraham's story, so here too there is no appearance of God, only a word (cf. Gen. 12.1; 13.14), or rather a twice-repeated call, to indicate an important, decisive revelation: 'Abraham, Abraham!' And immediately Abraham responds, 'Here I am' (*hinneni*), an extraordinary word that sums up his complete readiness to carry out God's will (cf. Luke 1.38). God's voice tells him: *Lekh lekha!* 'Go! Go towards yourself!' These are the same words that were addressed to Abraham in Genesis 12.1, with a parallelism that goes even further and includes the indication of a place; there it was a land, here it is a mountain in the land of Moriah. In short, Abraham is called to a new beginning, to start his journey again from scratch, to go to the roots of his vocation in order to repeat his prompt obedience to God.

Abraham knows well that obeying the Lord has meant fulfilling his own vocation, but now he is called to a new journey, even more obscure that the first. Indeed, it is no longer only a question of departing and giving up his links to his original family, but of offering in sacrifice his 37-year-old son.[3] This is the son of the promise, beloved by him, as the text makes insistently clear: 'your son, your only son Isaac, whom you love'. This man was able to renounce the ties of his past, but will he now also be able to renounce his intense bond with the future, his son Isaac? We must not forget that Isaac is a son given entirely by God, who 'did for Sarah as he had promised' (Gen. 21.1), carrying out what would have been humanly impossible for the elderly and sterile couple. On him depends Abraham's progeny, his future.

Carrying out the command

> Abraham rose early in the morning, saddled his donkey, and took two of his young men with him, and his son Isaac; he cut the wood for the burnt-offering, and set out and went to the place in the distance that God had shown him. On the third day Abraham looked up and saw the place far away.

Then Abraham said to his young men, 'Stay here with the donkey; the boy and I will go over there; we will worship, and then we will come back to you.' Abraham took the wood of the burnt-offering and laid it on his son Isaac, and he himself carried the fire and the knife. So the two of them walked on together. Isaac said to his father Abraham, 'Father!' And he said, 'Here I am, my son.' He said, 'The fire and the wood are here, but where is the lamb for a burnt-offering?' Abraham said, 'God himself will provide the lamb for a burnt-offering, my son.' So the two of them walked on together.

When they came to the place that God had shown him, Abraham built an altar there and laid the wood in order. He bound his son Isaac, and laid him on the altar, on top of the wood. Then Abraham reached out his hand and took the knife to kill his son. (Gen. 22.3–10)

After listening to God's command, Abraham makes no answer. He is silent, immersed in the deafening silence that enfolds his actions. He rises early in the morning, saddles his donkey, takes with him two servants and Isaac, chops the wood for the sacrifice and starts out on his journey towards the land of Moriah.[4] There is no word about the protagonists' feelings, but everything is described with extreme precision, almost as if in slow motion.

'On the third day Abraham looked up and saw the place far away.' Immediately after this comes the command to his servants to stop, so as to let him and his son go on. The encounter that is about to take place is to be between Abraham, Isaac and God, with no other witnesses, not even the donkey: 'The LORD will provide' (Gen. 22.14). In the last stage of climbing the mountain, while Isaac appears 'like one who carries the cross on his shoulders' (*Genesis Rabbah* 56.3; cf. Origen, *Homilies on Genesis* 8.6), father and son *walk on together*, an expression that recurs twice in the space of three verses. Father and son are fully in agreement with the sacrifice that will separate them for ever. Here there is a short conversation between them, a sparse dialogue in which Abraham again declares, 'Here I am.' Everything seems to be concentrated in the decisive question put by Isaac: 'Where is the lamb for a burnt-offering?' to which Abraham replies, 'God . . . will provide.' Is this an enigmatic response or does it suggest a more profound understanding of what is about to happen?

In the silence that returns to envelop the scene, the two reach the place indicated and events unfold rapidly. Abraham builds the altar, puts the wood on it, binds Isaac and places him on the altar on top of the wood. Everything is ready for the sacrifice. The tension is high, almost palpable, yet what is striking is the complete agreement of the two protagonists.

> Then came a voice from heaven: 'Come, look at the two persons united in a unique way. One sacrifices and the other is sacrificed; the one who sacrifices does not hesitate and the one who is sacrificed stretches out his throat.'
>
> (*Targum Neofiti* on Gen. 22.10)

Isaac shows himself completely obedient; he does not put up any resistance, he is not worried about himself. He is, so to speak, actively passive. Abraham performs the gestures that ratify his renunciation of God's gift; he is now disposed to give back promptly the son whom he had received by God's grace. Abraham, who felt that his son was bound up in his own being, now binds him on the altar and offers him to God. So Abraham in a ways cuts Isaac off from himself.

'Then Abraham reached out his hand and took the knife to kill his son.'

God's intervention

> But the angel of the LORD called to him from heaven, and said, 'Abraham, Abraham!' And he said, 'Here I am.' He said, 'Do not lay your hand on the boy or do anything to him; for now I know that you fear God, since you have not withheld your son, your only son, from me.' And Abraham looked up and saw a ram, caught in a thicket by its horns. Abraham

went and took the ram and offered it up as a burnt-offering instead of his son. So Abraham called that place, 'The LORD will provide'; as it is said to this day, 'On the mount of the LORD it shall be provided.'   (Gen. 22.11–14)

Abraham has shown himself obedient to the very end, and God's messenger intervenes and stops the act of sacrifice: again there is a repeated calling of his name, again his resolute 'Here I am'. The angel stays Abraham's arm with a word: 'Do not lay your hand on the boy.' Isaac has now become 'the boy';[5] his status as a son is only in relation to God. Abraham shows himself ready to listen to God even in that most fraught moment. From his heart, which is capable of listening, comes his swift observation that nearby is a ram entangled by its horns in a thicket; it can be offered in sacrifice. The narrator comments: 'Abraham called that place "The LORD will provide."' The Lord not only 'provides', he also 'sees': he sees Abraham's heart, he sees Isaac's heart and he intervenes in time.

The sacrifice has taken place but Isaac remains alive and Abraham finds his son again in a new way, as a son of God. That is why at the end of the story it is noted that Abraham 'returned to his young men' (Gen. 22.19) alone, without Isaac. Certainly the experience of Moriah put a distance between them and distinguished them. From that moment, Isaac is a son who can become a father and Abraham a father who recognizes that he must once again put all his hope in God, whose son he is: the God and Father of all, in short, 'Our Father' (Matt. 6.9).

The promise

The angel of the LORD called to Abraham a second time from heaven, and said, 'By myself I have sworn, says the LORD: Because you have done this, and have not withheld your son, your only son, I will indeed bless you, and I will make your offspring as numerous as the stars of heaven and as the sand that is on the seashore. And your offspring shall possess the gate of their enemies, and by your offspring shall all the

nations of the earth gain blessing for themselves, because
you have obeyed my voice.'   (Gen. 22.15–18)

The renewal of the promise addressed by God to Abraham in
favour of all humankind is based on a simple motivation, 'because
you have obeyed my voice', just as a short time before, the angel
said to him: 'Now I know that you fear God.' Did God need this
last test? Did he not have foreknowledge of Abraham's obedience?
Here too the apologists' explanations are not particularly helpful,
but I quote the two most useful:

> 'Now I know,' that is, 'now I make known to all that you love me.'
> (*Genesis Rabbah* 56.7)

> God already knew it, and it was not hidden from him, because
> he is 'aware of all things before they come to be' (Dan. 13.42).
> But it is written for you [the reader].[6]

No, it is not God who has put him to the test; rather, through
the event of the *'aqedah*, the binding, Abraham renewed his own
knowledge of God and learned to know God in a new way. Before
this episode, he counted on God as a trustworthy partner; after
it, he experiences the presence of a God in whom he has to believe
even in total darkness, even when he understands nothing about
him. 'From the God on whom he can count, whom he can use,
he passes gradually to the God who uses him.'[7]

Some interpretations

In the following pages I shall limit myself to discussing what seem
to me the most significant among the countless interpretations of
Genesis 22 offered over the years.[8]

The prohibition of human sacrifice

The first possible interpretation of Genesis 22 is the most traditional and the simplest from a historical point of view: this text
prohibits the practice of human sacrifice and institutes that of

animal sacrifice. The practice of the sacrifice of first-born children – well known in Greek mythology in the story of Agamemnon, who sacrifices his daughter Iphigenia in order to placate the gods – was normal for the people of Canaan among whom Israel came to live. It was also practised by the children of Israel (cf. 1 Kings 16.34; 2 Kings 3.26–27). The most striking case is that of Jephthah's daughter, sacrificed by her father in thanksgiving for his victory over his enemies (Judg. 11.29–40). In the Torah, God is thus forced to prohibit explicitly the offering of children to the god Molech.

> If the people of the land should ever close their eyes to them, when they give of their offspring to Molech, and do not put them to death, I myself will set my face against them and against their family, and will cut them off from among their people, them and all who follow them in prostituting themselves to Molech.
>
> (Lev. 20.4–5; cf. Deut. 12.31; 18.10; 2 Kings 23.10)

The God of Israel does not want these sacrifices and intervenes to stay the hand of the man who is ready to carry out such barbaric acts. Abraham mistakenly projected onto God an image formed by the dominant religious ideology, but God intervenes to enlighten the elderly patriarch and to induce him to desist from his foolish proposal. To sum up, Abraham had misunderstood God's word. This is what the midrash suggests with great finesse when it places these words in God's mouth: 'When I told you, "Take your son," I did not tell you "slay him" but "have him ascend". I told you this out of love and you made him ascend and carried out my command. Now have him descend.'[9]

Abraham's faith and obedience

According to the New Testament, this page of Genesis demonstrates Abraham's faith and obedience; he adheres to God without hesitation. We read in the Letter to the Hebrews:

> By faith Abraham, when put to the test, offered up Isaac. He who had received the promises was ready to offer up his only

son, of whom he had been told, 'It is through Isaac that descendants shall be named after you [Gen. 21.12]. He considered the fact that God is able even to raise someone from the dead – and figuratively speaking, he did receive him back.
(Heb. 11.17–19; cf. Jas. 2.21–23)

Reading between the lines of this passage, it appears that Abraham would in fact have sacrificed Isaac, thanks to his faith in the resurrection, the work of God par excellence. I will return to this shortly. Abraham is an extreme case, someone who passes the fundamental test, in which man shows what is in the depths of his heart. Abraham sees his own trust in God shaken to the foundations, through the night in which God seems to renege completely on his promises. In this event, he certainly experiences confusion, that is, the anguished state of one who no longer understands whether God is with him. He feels the dismay of one who loses the ability to make sense of his own existence, that situation in which the psalmist can only cry: 'In you, O LORD, I take refuge; let me never be put to shame' (Ps. 71.1).

Yet, confronted by this disastrous situation, while everything seems to go to pieces and his heart is broken (Ps. 51: *cor contritum*), Abraham continues to have faith in God, 'hoping against hope' (Rom. 4.18). Even if the features of God's face, familiar to him until that moment, seem to fade away, he perseveres in his faithful obedience to the same God, 'for he persevered as though he saw him who is invisible' (Heb. 11.27), despite a visible situation which in that moment seems only an incomprehensible contradiction and a painful denial.

Abraham goes through all this, yet remains firm. From that day on, it can truly be said that 'those who believe are the descendants of Abraham' (Gal. 3.7).

Jesus Christ, the new Isaac

The interpretation that is by far the most common among the Church fathers also merits a mention. It is typological: Jesus Christ is the new Isaac. Here are two of the many passages that could be quoted.

> It is said with regard to Our Lord Jesus Christ that 'he was bound like a ram' (cf. Gen. 22.13) and also that 'he was shorn like a sheep, led to slaughter like a lamb' (cf. Isa. 53.7). Indeed, he was crucified like a lamb and carried the wood on his shoulders, led to be sacrificed like Isaac by his father (cf. Gen. 22.6).... Isaac was a figure of him who was one day to suffer, Christ.[10]

> The Lord said, 'Your ancestor Abraham rejoiced that he would see my day; he saw it and was glad' (John 8.56). I think that here it refers to the day of the cross, prefigured by the sacrifice of the ram and of Isaac.[11]

The detail that modern exegesis has uncovered with a good measure of certainty should not be forgotten: Jesus underwent the crucifixion at the age of 37, Isaac's age at the time of the 'binding', according to tradition.

'Daddy, where are we going, just us?'

Finally, I would like to cite the interpretation of Genesis 22 contained in the *Midrash wa-yosha'*,[12] a splendid text of the Jewish tradition, which with great wisdom supplements the silences of the biblical account.

> It is written: 'Abraham rose early in the morning, saddled his donkey, and took two of his young men with him, and his son Isaac' (Gen. 22.3). Isaac said to his father: 'Daddy, where are we going, just us?' He said to him, 'My son, to a place nearby'. It is written: 'Abraham took the wood of the burnt-offering and laid it on his son Isaac, and he himself carried the fire and the knife. So the two of them walked on together' (Gen. 22.6) ... At once a great terror fell on Isaac because he saw nothing to be offered in sacrifice in his father's hands. And it is written: 'Isaac said to his father Abraham,

"Father!" And he said, "Here I am, my son." He said, "The fire and the wood are here, but where is the lamb for a burnt-offering?"' (Gen. 22.7) At once Isaac trembled and his hands shook because he understood his father's thought. He could not speak but forced himself to say to his father, 'If it is true that the Holy One has chosen me, then my life is given to him.' And Isaac accepted his death with peace, to carry out his Creator's command. Abraham said, 'My son, I know you will not oppose your Creator's command and mine.' Isaac replied to his father, 'My father, hurry! Carry out your Creator's will and he will carry out your will.'

After overcoming the wiles of Satan, who had tried to obstruct their journey by arousing doubts about what they were going to do, Abraham and Isaac

arrived at the place that God had told him. Here Abraham built the altar, put the wood on it, bound his son Isaac and placed him on the altar on top of the wood (Gen. 22.9). Abraham built the altar and Isaac handed him the wood and the stones. Abraham was like a man who is building a wedding chamber for his son, and Isaac was like a man who is preparing his nuptial bed and is doing it with joy. Isaac said, 'Daddy, be strong! Bare your arm and bind my hands and my feet well, because I am a youth of thirty-seven and you are old, so that when I see the knife in your hand I may not become agitated with fear and strike you, so that my soul may not rebel and I may not stain myself with the guilt of setting up any opposition, thus making myself unworthy of the sacrifice. I beg you then, Daddy, act quickly. Carry out your Creator's will, don't put it off!' . . . Immediately, Abraham laid the wood and bound Isaac on the altar on top of the wood. He braced his arm, rolled up his sleeves and put his knees on him with great force. The Holy One saw how the heart of each of them was the same. Tears sprang from Abraham and fell on Isaac, and from Isaac they fell on the wood, which was at once flooded with tears. 'Then Abraham reached out his hand and took the knife to kill his son' (Gen. 22.10). The Lord said to the angels-in-waiting: 'Did you see Abraham, my beloved, how he has borne witness to the oneness of my name in the world? If I had listened to you when at the creation of the world you said: "What are human beings that you are mindful of them, mortals that you care for them?" (Ps. 8.4), who would have confessed the oneness of my name like Abraham?' The angels-in-waiting wept and their tears fell on the knife, so that it was stopped and did not have strength on Isaac's neck, but immediately life left him. Then the Holy One said to Michael: 'Why are you standing still? Do not allow him to be killed!' Immediately, Michael called to Abraham and said: 'Do not lay your hand on the boy or do anything to him' (Gen. 22.11–12) . . . Abraham desisted and Isaac's life returned to him; he stood up and pronounced this benediction: 'Blessed are you, Lord, who give life to the dead.'

Besides its great poetic quality, this text is remarkable also for the detail about Isaac's resurrection, which constitutes a clear parallel to the Letter to the Hebrews. The connection between the *'aqedah* and the feast of the Passover, found in some works of the Jewish tradition (probably influenced by Christian reflections), runs along similar lines. 'Seeing the blood of the paschal lamb (cf. Exod. 12.13, 23),' says the Lord, 'I will see that of Isaac.'[13]

However, in my view the midrash holds an even more important teaching. Up to this moment, God had made a covenant with Abraham alone, but now Isaac also enters into the relationship between the two. Abraham no longer walks alone with God (cf. Gen. 17.1), but has to learn to keep pace with Isaac, just as Isaac has to do with regard to his father. 'The two of them walked on together' (Gen. 22.6, 8): together they carry the instruments for the sacrifice, together they prepare to carry it out. Their reciprocal obedience and their compassion reflect God's merciful face. God walks with man if man disposes himself to walk with the other, to be literally in concord, that is, animated by the same feeling, in daily mutual submission.

Conclusion

'The manifestation of the face is ethical.'[14] These words of Emmanuel Levinas summarize well the profound meaning of the text on which we have meditated. In Isaac's face, Abraham discerns the truth of the commandment 'You shall not murder' (Exod. 20.13; Deut. 5.17), and his hand, already stretched out in the sacrificial act, is as if paralysed. '"Abraham reached out his hand" (Gen. 22.10). He reached out his hand to take the knife and tears fell from his eyes, and the tears that sprang from his fatherly compassion fell on Isaac's eyes' (*Genesis Rabbah* 56.8).

Abraham is moved, and his tears are blended with Isaac's. When we suffer together, we realize that all violence is radically impossible. In fact, we come to realize that God cannot want death or any violent sacrifice, but only life in abundance (John 10.10) for all people. And this renewed knowledge of God is accompanied by another, more profound knowledge of oneself.

In this sense, Abraham's trial can be the lot of any one of us. It is a trial that is not willed by God but given to Abraham by history, because our poor human life can lead to such situations. Sooner or later, as believers, we realize that it is necessary to renounce what we hold most dear and on which we have based our life, in order to offer it promptly to God. Otherwise, our thinking becomes idolatrous, leading us to place our hope, not in God, but in his gift, which ends by becoming a stumbling block. Indeed, believers learn with difficulty to renounce freely every person, every relationship and all things, because nothing belongs to us. Paul will say: 'All belong to you, and you belong to Christ, and Christ belongs to God' (1 Cor 3.22–23).

I would like to end the reading of this difficult text with a suggestion. The love between Abraham and Isaac can evoke the concord between God and Jesus Christ. The Father did not want the Son's death, but accepted the fact that in an unjust world the righteous man can only be rejected and persecuted to the point of death (cf. Wisd. 1.16—2.24). In his turn, Jesus lives in full obedience to God's will, a will that asks that love be lived to the limit, even at the cost of going to a violent death. This reciprocal obedience leads to a free gesture born of a prodigal love: God recalls Jesus and has him rise from the dead, thus placing his seal on his whole life.

On Mount Golgotha, God's heart and Jesus' heart were closely united, as were Abraham's and Isaac's on Mount Moriah. 'An only beloved son in one case, an only beloved Son in the other.'[15] Truly, in Abraham, 'the father of all of us' (Rom. 4.16), we have a reflection of God's fatherhood, 'the Father, from whom every family in heaven and on earth takes its name' (Eph. 3.14–15).

3

*Jacob: the deceiver deceived,
the victor vanquished*

————••••————

May the Lord help me to explain such a great mystery: Jacob wrestles, he is the victor, but he wants to be blessed by him whom he himself has overcome.　　　　(Augustine, *Sermons* 5.6)

It is an obscure and disconcerting episode, the struggle by the Jabbok. In it, the protagonists have more than one name, the words mean more than one thing and every question leads to another . . . At dawn, Jacob is another man. Everything he touches bursts into flame . . . Did he win the fight? Can man overcome his own Creator? Naturally, it is impossible, but is it not a privilege to be overcome by God?

(Elie Wiesel, *Biblical Characters in the Midrash*)

We are still at the ford of Jabbok, and dawn has not yet come.

(Paolo de Benedetti, *Wrestling with the Angel*)

Introduction

'Abraham was the father of Isaac, and Isaac the father of Jacob' (Matt. 1.2). The cycle of events concerning Jacob, son of Isaac and Rebekah, Esau's twin, is to be found in chapters 22—35 of Genesis. It is quite an intriguing story and for this reason it has a great variety of rabbinic, patristic and contemporary interpretations.[1] In addition, it is a very human story, a turbulent and unedifying family affair, but it is through this that the promise of blessing for all humankind, addressed by God to Abraham (Gen. 12.1–3) and renewed to Isaac, is fulfilled.

To understand the figure of Jacob, it is necessary to begin with his parents, Isaac and Rebekah. A son's story is determined also by his father's and mother's, who bring him into the world and accompany him to adulthood. Everything begins with the intervention of God, who hears Isaac's prayer (Gen. 25.21). Sterile until that moment, Rebekah becomes pregnant with twins who 'struggled together within her' (Gen. 25.22), showing in embryo the rivalry that will characterize their whole lives. It should be noted that a twin birth constituted a real problem in a culture in which the first-born son enjoyed primacy over his brothers, signified by his inheriting the largest portion of his father's possessions. It was therefore necessary to determine with certainty which of the two twins was the first to come out of his mother's womb. Here, at the moment of birth, 'the first came out red, all his body like a hairy mantle; so they named him Esau. Afterwards his brother came out, with his hand gripping Esau's heel; so he was named Jacob' (Gen. 25.25–26). Already we have a glimpse of the future that awaits Jacob: he wants to prevent his twin from being the first-born and to do this tries to stop him by taking hold of his heel. The rabbinic tradition (see *Genesis Rabbah* 63.8) affirms that Jacob succeeded and was the first to come out of his mother's womb. This would of course vindicate his later claims, but it is an attempt to offer excuses for something unjustifiable. In reality, from his conception onwards, Jacob acts like a deceiver and this marks his name indelibly: *Ya'aqov*, related to the term *'aqev*, 'heel', but above all to the verb *'aqav*, 'to plot deceptions', as Esau will recall later (Gen. 27.36). The narrator then gives a sad detail about the family story as the two sons grow up. 'Isaac loved Esau, because he was fond of game; but Rebekah loved Jacob' (Gen. 25.28) and this second complicity will soon show itself.

At the beginning, Jacob is alone in pursuing his plans, astutely tricking Esau. The latter returns exhausted from hunting and, in exchange for a lentil soup which he consumes voraciously to satisfy his hunger, cedes to his brother the right of primogeniture (Gen. 25.29–34). When Isaac is old, blind and already near death, Rebekah suggests that Jacob steal his blessing from him by a stratagem. He puts on Esau's clothes, covers his arms and neck with goatskins, and in this way receives his father's irrevocable blessing (Gen. 27.1–29). It is a scandalous thing. In the religious tradition of Israel, the blessing is closely connected with righteousness and doing good; how then can it be received through deception? We should not interpret this episode as a sign of 'a still imperfect morality',[2] but rather assume the profound message that it contains. God's plan is fulfilled not in spite of Jacob's sin, but rather because of it. In other words, God is able to bring good even out of the evil freely done by man. Jacob betrays his father and deceives his brother with a calculated and evil plan, but once the sin is committed, God affirms the blessing of the guilty Jacob.

Nevertheless, Jacob will pay for it. He will atone for his guilt by a mysterious immanent justice due, not to God's punishment, but to the life events that will lead him to experience a simple truth: the deceiver is deceived. Jacob secured for himself the blessing that was Esau's due and took away from Isaac a son who was his true first-born, but the same thing will happen to him later, when his sons will take away Joseph, his favourite, and sell him as a slave (Gen. 37.12–30). Throughout his life it will be he, the deceiver, who will suffer deception. His uncle and father-in-law Laban will exploit him for seven years, promising him marriage to his beautiful daughter Rachel, with whom Jacob is madly in love, but on his wedding night he will find in his bed her sister Leah, a woman who is 'dull-eyed' (Gen. 29.17, NEB). To have a right to Rachel, Jacob will have to remain another seven years in Laban's service. Later his sons will deceive him, when they bring him Joseph's bloodstained clothes to make him believe that Joseph has been devoured by a wild beast (Gen. 37.31–36). In sum, there is a nemesis in deceit, an immanent justice that shows that in the long run it does not pay, or rather, the one who practises deception is repaid with deception.

Thus Jacob, having stolen the blessing from his brother, is forced – again on his mother's advice – to flee Esau's understandable anger. Like a coward, yet with his father's solemn blessing, he goes out from the land promised to Abraham and Isaac and goes to Mesopotamia, where he will seek work and a wife among Rebekah's relatives (Gen. 27.41—28.5). Jacob goes back towards Haran, the place from which Abraham had gone out at the beginning of salvation history (see Gen. 12.4). And just as he is journeying as a stranger at the borders of the promised land, the first of his two decisive encounters with God occurs. These are enigmatic meetings that tell the story of his own 'salvation history'.

Jacob's dream

Jacob left Beer-sheba and went towards Haran. He came to a certain place[3] and stayed there for the night, because the sun had set. Taking one of the stones of the place, he put it under his head and lay down in that place. And he dreamed that there was a ladder set up on the earth, the top of it reaching to heaven; and the angels of God were ascending and descending on it.[4] And the LORD stood beside him[5] and said, 'I am the LORD, the God of Abraham your father and the God of Isaac; the land on which you lie I will give to you and to your offspring; and your offspring shall be like the dust of the earth, and you shall spread abroad to the west and to the east and to the north and to the south; and all the families of the earth shall be blessed in you and in your offspring. Know that I am with you and will keep you wherever you go, and will bring you back to this land; for I will not leave you until I have done what I have promised you.' Then Jacob woke from his sleep and said, 'Surely the LORD is in this place – and I did not know it!' And he was afraid, and said, 'How awesome is this place! This is none other than the house of God, and this is the gate of heaven.'

So Jacob rose early in the morning, and he took the stone that he had put under his head and set it up for a pillar and poured oil on the top of it. He called that place Bethel; but the name of the city was Luz at the first. Then Jacob made a vow, saying, 'If God will be with me, and will keep me in this way that I go, and will give me bread to eat and clothing to wear, so that I come again to my father's house in peace, then the LORD shall be my God, and this stone, which I have set up for a pillar, shall be God's house; and of all that you give me I will surely give one-tenth to you.'

(Gen. 28.10–22)

Up to this point in his life, Jacob has appeared as anything but one who seeks God. He had not met him, but had striven to obtain advantages for himself at all costs. Here now is the unexpected novelty: on the frontier of the promised land, it is God who goes to meet Jacob and shows himself to him. Everything happens during the night, the mysterious hour par excellence, when Jacob, having arrived at an unspecified place, has lain down, using a stone for a pillow. Having fallen asleep, he dreams of a ladder, that is, a ziggurat, a series of steps like those of Mesopotamian temples that aimed to ascend to heaven. This stairway rests on the ground but does reach heaven, and on it ascend and descend the angels of God. More importantly, 'the LORD stood beside him' (Gen. 28.13).

It is known that in antiquity a dream was an event connected with a message from God; it was considered to be a means through which God chose to raise the veil that covered him and so enter into communion with human beings.[6] From the perspective of the biblical account, it seems to me that the simplest interpretation of Jacob's dream is that communication between God and man, between heaven and earth, is possible and occurs by God's initiative. In other words, here it is not a case of the ziggurat of Babel (see Gen. 11.1–9), a 'gate of God' built by humans to grasp at divinity and seize heaven, but a ladder that God willed and freely offered so that his Presence might be communicated to them. After all, the angels, God's messengers, represent God's energy, his action in the heart of humanity, on earth and in history. The dream says that there is a path walked by God, who wishes to enter into relationship with people 'to offer them his marvellous gifts'.[7]

Thus God goes before Jacob; he shows himself as the God of his fathers and confirms to him the blessing made to Abraham and renewed to Isaac, making him the bearer of the promise. In this way, Jacob experiences that God was already present and waiting for him, because his love is always anticipatory, well beyond human awareness. 'The LORD is in this place – and I did not know it!' (Gen. 28.16). The ability to notice God's passage through one's life is almost always retrospective. His traces, his 'back' (Exod. 33.23) are noticeable, but one cannot endure being face to face with him. Moreover, God surprises Jacob in order to make himself known by him as his God. 'I am with you' (Gen. 28.15). Jacob confesses God as the God of those who preceded him, whose name is transmitted from father to son, but he has to manage to see him as the God of his own personal life. Until he can reach the point of saying, like Abraham, 'O Lord GOD' (Gen. 15.2, 8 etc.), he will be far from able to communicate authentically with the Lord.

It cannot be overemphasized that in this wearisome journey it is God who takes the initiative. In this episode, God reveals himself to Jacob with a word of

- *self-representation*: 'I am the LORD, the God of Abraham your father and the God of Isaac';
- *promise*: 'the land on which you lie I will give to you and to your offspring; and your offspring shall be like the dust of the earth';
- *blessing*: 'all the families of the earth shall be blessed in you and in your offspring';
- *covenant*: 'I am with you and will keep you wherever you go, and will bring you back to this land; for I will not leave you.'

On waking, Jacob is greatly disturbed because he was not prepared for the night's experience. When he overcomes his surprise and fear, he decides to set up the stone used as his pillow and to anoint it permanently, so that it may become a memorial to his encounter with God. At the same time, he feels the need to change the name of the place where he was and calls it Bethel, 'house of God'. Finally,

Jacob responds to God's revelation with a vow, committing his own future to God without delay (see Gen. 28.20–22).

After this first encounter with God, Jacob appears to be on the way to being transformed into what is essential. Whereas, until that night, he had intended to be the master of his own life, he now begins to know a God who prepares the future and who accompanies him as he lives out his personal life. Jacob will no longer be the cunning deceiver but a person who trusts in the word received from God. He will seek to live in faithfulness to the covenant that now binds him to the God of his fathers, who has become his God.

Jacob's wrestling

After living with Laban for 20 years (see Gen. 31.38, 41), Jacob, married to Rachel and Leah and father of 11 sons, prepares to return to the land of Canaan. Although a great deal of time has passed, he knows he will have to square accounts with Esau, whom he has deceived and dispossessed. Fearing revenge, he sends several peace envoys ahead of him. Informed by them that Esau is approaching with 400 men, he divides his caravan into two parts, in the hope that at least part of them will be saved. Then, in a last attempt at reconciliation, he entrusts a servant with some choice animals to offer as a gift to his brother. 'For he thought, "I may appease him with the present that goes ahead of me, and afterwards I shall see his face; perhaps he will accept me"' (Gen. 32.20). Here are traces of his old cunning.

It is in this context that Jacob fights a truly unique nocturnal battle. Here is the passage that narrates this experience of an abyss:

> The same night he got up and took his two wives, his two maids, and his eleven children, and crossed the ford of the Jabbok. He took them and sent them across the stream, and likewise everything that he had. Jacob was left alone; and a man wrestled with him until daybreak. When the man saw

that he did not prevail against Jacob, he struck him on the hip socket; and Jacob's hip was put out of joint as he wrestled with him. Then he said, 'Let me go, for the day is breaking.' But Jacob said, 'I will not let you go, unless you bless me.' So he said to him, 'What is your name?' And he said, 'Jacob.' Then the man said, 'You shall no longer be called Jacob, but Israel, for you have striven with God and with humans, and have prevailed.' Then Jacob asked him, 'Please tell me your name.' But he said, 'Why is it that you ask my name?' And there he blessed him. So Jacob called the place Peniel, saying, 'For I have seen God face to face, and yet my life is preserved.' The sun rose upon him as he passed Penuel, limping because of his hip. Therefore to this day the Israelites do not eat the thigh muscle that is on the hip socket, because he struck Jacob on the hip socket at the thigh muscle.

(Gen. 32.22–32)

Once again it is night, a time of insecurity when one is not in control of time and space. Night is the absence of light and, at the same time, a necessary passage through the darkness to the light, a womb in which the sun prepares to shine anew. Jacob experiences total solitude, a condition that is the absence of others, so as to be completely himself. This makes him responsible for others; it is a crucible that permits the full assumption of his own uniqueness, enabling him to form truly conscious relationships.

In this situation 'a man [*ish*] wrestled with him' (Gen. 32.24), rolling with him in the dust.[8] He, who from the very womb of his mother had taken part in strenuous struggles, comes upon another who attacks him. It is another man, not identified and unknown to Jacob. He was awaiting the encounter and possible confrontation with Esau and instead is surprised and forestalled by someone who throws him to the ground. Here we have a formidable struggle, the intertwining of two bodies that embrace and strike each other. The Hebrew text expresses this hand-to-hand combat by a succession of short phrases, the subject of which is not specified. A better way to convey this than words are the many and varied artistic representations that over the centuries have interpreted this episode: hieratic struggle in Byzantine iconography, a resistant embrace in Rembrandt, the collision of two powerful bodies in Eugène Delacroix, an ambiguous embrace between an old man and a youth in Morazzone, a collision between an imposing angel and a tiny Jacob in Marc Chagall. Jacob wrestles with an unnamed man, with his own shadow, with an angel who represents his own double, with Esau's guardian angel and, as we shall see, wrestles with God.[9]

In any case, he shows himself to be a tenacious, indomitable wrestler, to the point that his antagonist, seeing 'that he did not prevail against Jacob . . . struck him on the hip socket; and Jacob's hip was put out of joint' (Gen. 32.25). We are in the midst of a fight with no holds barred, in which there is no hesitation in hitting below the belt! Only at the end of the night does Jacob hear his rival say: 'Let me go, for the day is breaking' (Gen. 32.26). This is the hour in which shadows flee and God shines out as salvation. But Jacob does not let go at once, and there is an excited dialogue between the two contenders. Jacob asks the other for his blessing but is answered with the question: 'What is your name?' (Gen. 32.27). And so Jacob surrenders to his adversary because to give one's own name means an explicit giving of oneself. The name is the person, the most intimate reality of every human being, and Jacob, in giving it, commits himself.

While he does this, there is another surprise: his own name is changed: 'You shall no longer be called Jacob, but Israel, for you have striven with God and with humans, and have prevailed' (Gen. 32.28). Who can change one's name if not God (see Gen. 17.5, 15)? Jacob, who has not yet realized who his interlocutor is, in his turn asks him his name and hears himself answered with a blessing. But is not a blessing itself God's name? In invoking God's blessing, surely one invokes the Presence of him whose name cannot be uttered? At this point, Jacob-Israel, conscious of having

37

seen God face to face, in his turn changes the name of the place. Finally, he goes away limping, while the sun rises over him (Gen. 32.31–32). Rereading this page, Hosea will write: 'In the womb [Jacob] tried to supplant his brother, and in his manhood he strove with God. He strove with the angel and prevailed, he wept and sought his favour' (Hos. 12.3–4).[10] Jacob is a winner who weeps and asks for mercy; he is a wounded winner, that is, he shows in his body that in reality God has prevailed against him and in him. Jacob is a defeated winner. Lame and weeping, he is no longer the man he was before, the deceiver, but he is now a wrestler who by grace has received a blessing. He is a new man with a new name, *Yisra'el*, the name of the people of the covenant and of the blessings. In that struggle he consigned to God his entire life, including his sin and his lies, receiving in exchange a new 'birth from above' (cf. John 3.3), not from his mother's womb.

Jacob's struggle is deeply disturbing and a metaphor for every human struggle with God. Sooner or later, all human beings experience their own confrontation with God. It is not possible and perhaps not even right to establish the causes of this struggle with God, or the precise ways in which it unfolds. What counts is the experience, and everyone knows it in a very personal form. At times God seems to be silent, unable to carry out his promise. But is he really silent, or do human beings just not know how to listen? Does he hide himself, or do human beings not believe him to be present? The struggle with God is like birth pangs, the prelude to a new birth. That is why God asks Jacob: 'What is your name?' (Gen. 32.27). It is the same question that his father Isaac addressed to him, to which he replied: 'I am Esau' (Gen. 27.19), in order to steal the blessing. Jacob had lived in falsehood and deceit and now God questions him, so as to bring him to the truth: 'And he said, "Jacob"' (Gen. 32.27). Only at this point is his rebirth possible. 'You shall no longer be called Jacob, but Israel, for you have striven with God and with humans, and have prevailed' (Gen. 32.28). He is a victorious wrestler, a winner who has become lame and will carry for ever the marks of his struggle.

And yet, *Yisra'el* means literally 'God fights, God is strong', the exact opposite of the explanation given by our text.[11] So then, in the struggle with God, who overcomes and who is overcome? It is a difficult question to answer. It is enough to examine the evidence of the long road travelled by this man as he passes from being 'he who deceives' to becoming Israel, 'God is strong'. With his tormented history, Jacob bears witness to the necessity of struggling with oneself so as to be ready to receive God's presence in everything. This involves conflict with the other, one's brother, in relationship, as a night struggle awaiting the dawn, alternately locked in an embrace and thrust apart. It involves struggling with the Other, who is God, trying to hold on to him even in the hour of darkness, certain that the blessing will come sooner or later. God, in fact, overcomes only with love, and relationship with him demands the wound of love.

'And there he blessed him' (Gen. 32.29). After the blow to his hip, when Jacob was overcome, he becomes the victor. He can now receive the blessing and can also give a new name to the place: *Peniel*, 'face of God', saying, 'I have seen God face to face, and yet my life is preserved' (Gen. 32.30). Jacob at last understands that God's blessing is a free gift; it cannot be exchanged, stolen or seized. In this struggle, Jacob becomes the one who is blessed freely by God; in fact, he becomes a bearer of blessing to such an extent that he will no longer be able to keep it for himself. He will bless each of his sons with a particular blessing (Gen. 49); he will even bless Pharaoh (Gen. 47.7, 10), the *goy* par excellence. Jacob is blessed so that all peoples may be blessed. He too, through his troubled story, will fulfil God's plan: blessing for all humankind.

Conclusion

After his dream, but especially after wrestling in the night, Jacob, as we have said, is no longer the same. This man's story, however, contains a more profound and fundamental lesson: after the struggle with God, God, too, is not the same as before. In this blessed but costly struggle, another face of God is revealed. In Job's words, 'I had heard of you by the hearing of the ear, but now my eye sees you' (Job 42.5). Moreover, if we listen deeply to Jacob's story, we understand that God always remains faithful to his promise, a promise that is rendered null and void for those who want to 'force' it or to seize it for themselves. Instead, we have to submit freely to his absolute gratuitousness, allowing it to be fulfilled in its time.

Finally, Jacob's struggle reveals that there is an enigma also in God. It is an enigma that is part of human faith, which is always tempted to incredulity. It saves God from being reduced to an idol that can be manipulated and exploited at one's pleasure, and saves faith from presuming to understand and solve every problem. Faith is not a peaceful adventure; sometimes it is a fight with no holds barred, whose outcome is never known with certainty. We can understand why, when Paul came to the end of his life, he felt the need to affirm: 'I have fought the good fight, I have finished the race, I have kept the faith' (2 Tim 4.7).

One thing, however, is certain: after this struggle, nothing is the same as before. The prospective of a new life opens up. Then God's promise is finally fulfilled, not one's own projects or one's imagined vocation.

4

Moses and the name of God

How is it that the man to whom God showed himself through numerous theophanies – 'the Lord used to speak to Moses face to face, as one speaks to a friend' (Exod. 33.11) – how is it that he asks God to show himself to him? (Exod. 33.18)? . . . Moses, always straining forward, does not put a limit to his ascent but, once he has set his foot on the ladder 'on the top of which is God' (cf. Gen. 28.12), he does not cease to rise, step by step . . . He burns with desire and still thirsts for that of which he has drunk his fill.

> (Gregory of Nyssa, *Life of Moses* 2.219, 227, 230)

To discover everything that God can expect of a human being, it is necessary to read the Bible story of Moses.

> (Paul Beauchamp, *Fifty Biblical Portraits*)

The Holy One, blessèd be he, kissed Moses and took away his breath with a kiss of his mouth.

> (*Deuteronomy Rabbah* 11.10)

Introduction

The figure of Moses is present in all the books of the Torah from Genesis to Exodus to Deuteronomy, and his encounters with God are undoubtedly unique.[1] Only of him, in fact, does the Bible say that 'the Lord used to speak to Moses face to face, as one speaks to a friend' (Exod. 33.11; cf. Num. 12.8; Deut. 34.10). With Moses, we see the fullness of encounter with God in the Old Testament, a fullness that fulfils and at the same time transcends the knowledge of God experienced by Abraham, Isaac and Jacob.

The book of Exodus, in particular, records two meetings of Moses with God in which God reveals his own name: Moses' call (Exod. 3.1–15) and the encounter in which the covenant is renewed, after the children of Israel had sinned in making the golden calf (Exod. 33.18—34.9). The first meeting is the foundation of the second, the second a development of the first.

Ehyeh asher ehyeh

From the moment of his birth, Moses experiences in his own person Pharaoh's persecution of the children of Israel, but is saved from the waters of the Nile thanks to the intervention of Pharaoh's daughter (Exod. 2.1–10). Once grown up, after fleeing Egypt following the act of violence by which he had tried to restore justice (Exod. 2.11–15), Moses stays in the land of Midian, a territory situated beyond the Red Sea in the Arabian Peninsula. Here he marries one of the daughters of Jethro, the priest of Midian, and takes up the life of a shepherd (Exod. 2.16–22). The narrator notes:

> After a long time the king of Egypt died. The Israelites groaned under their slavery, and cried out. Out of the slavery their cry for help rose up to God. God heard their groaning, and God remembered his covenant with Abraham, Isaac, and Jacob. God looked upon the Israelites, and God took notice of them.
>
> (Exod. 2.23–25)

It is at this point that Moses encounters God for the first time.

> Moses was keeping the flock of his father-in-law Jethro, the priest of Midian; he led his flock beyond the wilderness, and came to Horeb, the mountain of God. There the angel of the Lord appeared to him in a flame of fire out of a bush; he looked, and the bush was blazing, yet it was not consumed. Then Moses said, 'I must turn aside and look at this great sight, and see why the bush is not burned up.' When the Lord saw that he had turned aside to see, God called him out of the bush, 'Moses, Moses!' And he said, 'Here I am.' Then he

said, 'Come no closer! Remove the sandals from your feet, for the place on which you are standing is holy ground.' He said further, 'I am the God of your father, the God of Abraham, the God of Isaac, and the God of Jacob.' And Moses hid his face, for he was afraid to look at God.

Then the LORD said, 'I have observed the misery of my people who are in Egypt; I have heard their cry on account of their taskmasters. Indeed, I know their sufferings, and I have come down to deliver them from the Egyptians, and to bring them up out of that land to a good and broad land, a land flowing with milk and honey, to the country of the Canaanites, the Hittites, the Amorites, the Perizzites, the Hivites, and the Jebusites. The cry of the Israelites has now come to me; I have also seen how the Egyptians oppress them. So come, I will send you to Pharaoh to bring my people, the Israelites, out of Egypt.' But Moses said to God, 'Who am I that I should go to Pharaoh and bring the Israelites out of Egypt?' He said, 'I will be with you; and this shall be the sign for you that it is I who sent you: when you have brought the people out of Egypt, you shall worship God on this mountain.'

But Moses said to God, 'If I come to the Israelites and say to them, "The God of your ancestors has sent me to you", and they ask me, "What is his name?" what shall I say to them?' God said to Moses, 'I AM WHO I AM.' He said further, 'Thus you shall say to the Israelites, "I AM has sent me to you."' God also said to Moses, 'Thus you shall say to the Israelites, "The LORD, the God of your ancestors, the God of Abraham, the God of Isaac, and the God of Jacob, has sent me to you": This is my name for ever, and this my title for all generations.'   (Exod. 3.1–15)

Moses is performing his ordinary daily task, leading the animals to pasture. When he reaches Mount Horeb, suddenly 'the angel', that is, the messenger 'of the LORD appeared to him in a flame of fire out of a bush' (Exod. 3.2). It is always God who takes the initiative in meeting with mortals; it is he who first calls and chooses to meet them. Humans can respond only through the obedience of faith, pronouncing the word that better than any other expresses their readiness to listen to the God who goes before them: 'Here I am' (cf. Gen. 22.1, 11; 31.11; 46.2). And yet this sudden appearance of God in Moses' life cannot but provoke in him, as in every human being, astonishment, fear and trembling. Humans are 'afraid to look at God' (cf. Exod. 3.6), feeling inadequate and sinful, incapable of standing in the presence of God's holiness, his absolute otherness. Nothing is more foreign to humankind than the divine.

God himself, however, bridges the distance between himself and Moses and presents himself to him. 'I am the God of your father, the God of Abraham, the God of Isaac, and the God of Jacob' (Exod. 3.6). He reveals himself as the God of the generations that preceded Moses, the God already known to the Hebrews under the name of *El, Elohim*. Before being 'his God', he is the God of those who went before him. Because they handed on the faith, God can manifest his marvels from generation to generation. He is the God who made a covenant with Abraham, Isaac and Jacob, and with Moses' own father; as Jesus will say, he is 'God not of the dead, but of the living' (Mark 12.27 and parallels). As Deuteronomy reveals, our God is a God who speaks (cf. Deut. 4.32–33) and a God who loves (cf. Deut. 7.7–8), because he knows the suffering of his people (cf. Exod. 2.25; 3.7–9). It is to speak to his people and to free them from slavery that God reveals himself to Moses and enters into dialogue with him, entrusting him with a mission of liberation. 'So come, I will send you to Pharaoh to bring my people, the Israelites, out of Egypt' (Exod. 3.10).

Moses, surprised, objects to God: 'Who am I that I should go to Pharaoh, and bring the Israelites out of Egypt?' (Exod. 3.11). We should not forget that later on Moses will be described as 'very humble, more so than anyone else on the face of the earth' (Num. 12.3). Here, however, Moses' question probably expresses awkwardly a very human fear in the face of the demanding task proposed to him. But God is not discouraged and repeats his proposal to Moses with words that should have reassured him definitively: 'I will be with you' (Exod. 3.12). This is the promise already made to Abraham (Gen. 17.4, 7), Isaac (Gen. 26.3, 24) and Jacob (Gen. 28.15; 31.3). It is the fundamental experience of faith, a faith born of listening to and accepting God's word. This is the essential element of the relationship between human beings and God, namely, the capacity to recognize God as 'Immanuel', that is, God-with-us (Isa. 7.14; 8.8, 10; cf. Matt. 1.23). Moses, however, is not yet satisfied. He wants to know God's own name, the name that identifies the God of his fathers personally. The mystery of the name is great. Today its significance is no longer understood, but in antiquity there was a clear awareness that the name expresses the profound truth about a person. A name is what permits knowledge and communication, much more than saying 'you'. Here is God's response, articulated in three successive affirmations:

- *Ehyeh asher ehyeh.*
- 'You shall say to the Israelites, "I AM [*Ehyeh*] has sent me to you."'
- 'You shall say to the Israelites, "The LORD, the God of your ancestors, the God of Abraham, the God of Isaac, and the God of Jacob, has sent me to you": This is my name for ever, and this my title for all generations.'

Ehyeh asher ehyeh. Much ink has been spilt on the subject of this name, not all of it relevant. Its literal translation could be: 'I AM WHO I AM' or 'I will be who I will be', but there are other interpretations. Certainly this is not a definition of God's ontological essence, as some have thought, on the basis of the Greek version of these words: 'I am Being' (*egó eimi ho ón*). As we shall see later, it is probably a way of affirming the Lord's loving nearness to Moses and the children of Israel, already expressed to Moses in the words: 'I will be with you' (Exod. 3.12). The interpretation given by the great medieval commentator Rashi of Troyes is along these lines. 'I shall be with the children of Israel in this misfortune. I shall be with them in their slavery.'[2] Not by chance, the name is immediately repeated in connection with Moses' mission: 'Thus you shall say to the Israelites, "I AM [*Ehyeh*] has sent me to you."' After these three enigmatic words comes the ineffable name, the tetragram YHWH, derived from a Hebrew root that means 'to be, to become, to work, to show oneself efficacious'. With the death of the last high priest and the destruction of the Jerusalem Temple, the knowledge of how these consonants were vocalized was lost. Since then, it has been the convention to read this word as if it were *Adonai*, 'my Lord' (cf. *b. Pesahim* 50a). We know, however, that on the occasion of Yom Kippur, the Day of Atonement, the high priest within the holy of holies pronounced the Lord's name, in which the people received the remission of their sins and thus experienced renewed communion with God (cf. *b. Yoma* 66a). In fact, the revelation of the name and the action of liberation and salvation are all one, because 'God is called according to his acts' (*Exodus Rabbah* 3.6): 'the LORD, the God of your ancestors' (Exod. 3.15) is for all time the 'God of salvation' (Ps. 68.20). In this sense, his name is a memorial, an efficacious, dynamic and living memory from generation to generation.

Moses was able to know the very name of the God of his ancestors. What had been refused to Jacob (Gen. 32.29) is given to him and he in his turn will pass it on to the people. Nevertheless, the mystery of the name remains. Something of it, a sign or trace, is known but cannot be pronounced with certainty because the Lord God cannot be confined within a definition.

'I will make all my goodness pass before you, and will proclaim before you the name'

Moses carried out his mission, bringing Israel out of Egypt, and the covenant was celebrated at Sinai, on the basis of the Decalogue (Exod. 20.1–21), sealed by the promise: 'Everything that the LORD has spoken we will do' (Exod. 19.8; 24.7). Encouraged by Aaron, the people afterwards fall into the great sin of making the golden calf. Since Moses takes his time coming down the mountain, the children of Israel forge for themselves an idol of molten metal and worship it (Exod. 32.1–9). The consequence of this is the breaking off of the covenant, sanctioned by the act of Moses who, having come down from Sinai, breaks the two tablets of the covenant by hurling them to the ground.

Then Moses burns with anger and, without receiving a command from God, has 3,000 Levites killed (Exod. 32.25–29). God's anger has been placated through the supplication of Moses, who had struggled with God, placing himself on the side of the sinful people 'against' God himself (Exod. 32.11–14). Immediately afterwards, however, the same Moses decides to punish the people. The paradoxical truth is that God pardons but Moses will not. Later on, Moses will again intercede with God in favour of his people in extremely strong terms ('If you will only forgive their sin . . . if not, blot me out of the book that you have written' (Exod. 32.32). But here he is prey to evil zeal, which leads him to carry out a terrible massacre. He who, when angry, spoke without reflection (cf. Ps. 106.33), here allows himself to be drawn to a terrible deed. Perhaps this is the grave sin for which the Lord will stop Moses from entering the promised land.

After this sad interlude, Moses continues to converse with God in the 'tent of meeting' (Exod. 27.21; 28.43 etc.) at every stage of the journey, and the Lord speaks to him 'face to face – clearly, not in riddles' (Num. 12.8). Thus Moses grows in his desire to know the Lord better and be in relationship with him. 'If I have found favour in your sight, show me your ways, so that I may know you and find favour in your sight' (Exod. 33.13). A little later he addresses to God 'the bold request that goes beyond the bounds of desire':[3] 'Show me your glory' (Exod. 33.18).[4]

To see the face of God and his glory is the deep desire of every human being. This yearning is voiced by Moses, who asks to be able to catch sight of that splendour of God which human beings are able to perceive. He asks to see God himself, just as he is known by God. God, however, does not seem to respond exactly to this request. He says, in fact:

'I will make all my goodness pass before you, and will proclaim before you the name, "The LORD"; and I will be gracious to whom I will be gracious, and will show mercy on whom I will show mercy. But', he said, 'you cannot see my face; for no one shall see me and live.' And the LORD continued, 'See, there is a place by me where you shall stand on the rock; and while my glory passes by I will put you in a cleft of the rock, and I will cover you with my hand until I have passed by; then I will take away my hand, and you shall see my back; but my face shall not be seen.' (Exod. 33.19–23)

Moses had asked to see God's glory but the Lord shows him his goodness (*tuv*), his love. God's glory and goodness, therefore, are identical. Here we have a virtual declaration that God's transcendence and holiness consist in his goodness. This prevents God from disowning the Israelites in spite of their sin; it enjoins forgiveness and attests to the victory of love over justice. God will say through another prophet, Hosea:

How can I give you up, Ephraim? How can I hand you over, O Israel?
. . . My heart recoils within me; my compassion grows warm and tender. I will not execute my fierce anger; I will not again destroy Ephraim; for I am God and no mortal, the Holy One in your midst, and I will not come in wrath.
(Hos. 11.8–9)

Indeed, God's transcendence lies in his capacity to forgive. Human beings find this hard, but God is omnipotent in loving. Here we see the revelation that will be completed in the New Testament, above all thanks to the meditation of the apostle John. 'God is love' (1 John 4.8, 16), and Jesus Christ has borne witness to God in his human life. Jesus reveals the glory of him who loves his brothers and sisters and gives his life for them (cf. John 15.13), the glory of him who pardons his enemy, a sinner, a persecutor and even a murderer (cf. Luke 23.34).

God's answer shows that he was able to understand the desire that had inspired Moses' request – to find out whether God is really capable of pardoning. He wants to discover whether God accepts being in a covenant relationship with a sinful, 'stiff-necked' people (Exod. 32.9; 33.3, 5; 34.9), whether he can unilaterally renew the covenant broken by the people without punishing them as Moses had just done. As for his way of revealing himself, God is an elusive Presence, which shows itself in passing. God visits fleetingly, in a moment of grace, in a *kairós* that should not be allowed to go by in vain, and he does this without ever definitively unveiling his face. In this passage, the Lord's name that Moses had heard in the encounter of the burning bush is spoken again in a different way. 'I AM WHO I AM' (Exod. 3.14) becomes 'I will be gracious to whom I will be gracious,[5] and will show mercy on whom I will show mercy' (Exod. 33.19). The parallelism is evident, but there is a shift from a state of being to the action of God's love.[6] God is 'he who is' before Pharaoh and before Egypt in his act of liberation; he is 'the one who acts with favour and mercy' towards the sinner, offering his salvation to every human being. God loves human beings with a gratuitous and merciful love; he is the Father who loves with maternal tenderness.

In other words, what can be seen of God here on earth is his love. Everything else will be revealed after death, when we will 'see [him] face to face' (1 Cor. 13.12). Besides, God does not say to Moses that he will hide his face, but very delicately promises him that he will cover him with his hand until he has passed by. Thus Moses will see his back (Exod. 33.23: *posteriora mea*, according to Jerome's picturesque translation), his footsteps. Moses talked directly to God but without seeing his face, because the experience of God that a human being can have is always partial, and, more-over, God does not let himself be reduced to a visual image.[7]

'The LORD, the LORD . . . merciful and gracious'

In chapter 34 of Exodus there is the encounter promised by God. It is a theophany, a renewal of the covenant. At the Lord's command, Moses ascends Mount Sinai alone, carrying with him two stone tablets.

> The LORD descended in the cloud and stood with him there, and proclaimed[8] the name, 'The LORD.' The LORD passed before him, and proclaimed, 'The LORD [YHWH], the LORD [YHWH], a God [*El*] merciful and gracious, slow to anger, and abounding in steadfast love and faithfulness, keeping steadfast love for the thousandth generation, forgiving [literally, 'carrying'] iniquity and transgression and sin, yet by no means clearing the guilty, but visiting the iniquity of the parents upon the children and the children's children, to the third and fourth generation.' And Moses quickly bowed his head toward the earth, and worshipped. He said, 'If now I have found favour in your sight, O Lord, I pray, let the Lord go with us. Although this is a stiff-necked people, pardon our iniquity and our sin, and take us for your inheritance.' (Exod. 34.5–9)

This proclamation of the Lord's name recapitulates the previous encounters between God and Moses; it marks a further revelation and, at least within the Old Testament, constitutes the definitive interpretation of the face of God as a face of love. The revelation of the name in Exodus 34.6–7, known in the Hebrew tradition as the 'covenant of the 13 attributes', has been the subject of countless commentaries both within the Bible itself (cf. Num. 14.18; Deut. 7.9–10 and others) and by rabbis and Church fathers. As I follow in the wake of many exegetes, I would merely like to stress some fundamental points.

First of all, it should be noted that it does not say that Moses invoked the Lord's name and then the Lord descended, but the two events are placed the opposite way around. Moses responds to God, who always comes to seek him first. The passage opens with a double repetition of the tetragram, in this way tying up with Exodus 3.15. It could also be translated: 'YHWH is YHWH, a God merciful and gracious . . .' The essential thing about the Lord's name is the disproportion between the 11 attributes of mercy and the last two of justice. Mercy has a price and it would not be mercy if it were separated from justice, but what an imbalance! The human difficulty in defining God's merciful and compassionate acts is clearly illustrated by the 'pious lie' of verse 7, an affirmation that goes against all logic and common sense: '[The LORD keeps] steadfast love for the thousandth generation . . . but [visits] the iniquity of the parents upon the children and the children's children, to the third and the fourth generation.' In short, God is in no hurry to punish; rather in his *macrothymia*, or magnanimity, he is patient and slow to anger. Jeremiah (Jer. 15.15), Jonah (Jonah 4.2–3) and many others will complain of this slowness of God; they will consider it unbearable, failing to understand that in this very patience lies his power, not his weakness. The Lord acts in this way because he is 'abounding in steadfast love and faithfulness' (Exod. 34.6: *rav chesed we-emeth*), because 'his steadfast love endures for ever', as Psalm 136 sings.

When he heard this name, 'Moses quickly bowed his head towards the earth, and worshipped' (Exod. 34.8). Then he shows that he has a profound understanding of the revelation he has just received. He asks that the Lord pardon the people's sin, with which he once again associates himself, repeating the request made before (Exod. 32.32). The Lord grants this and his pardon results in the renewal of the covenant (Exod. 34.10–28). Then Moses comes down from the mountain with his face shining and transfigured, yet has to cover it with a veil when he speaks to the children of Israel because they are afraid of him (Exod. 34.29–35). This detail certainly expresses the grace that God has given to Moses, but I believe it can also be understood in another way. Now that Moses has known and communicated God's love to the people, the people no longer have to gaze on the face of the one who punished them, but can address God directly, the God who always forgives and who will be able to make a unilateral covenant through his Son Jesus Christ (cf. Rom. 5.6–11).

The Prologue of John's Gospel concludes with the affirmation: 'No one has ever seen God. It is God the only Son, who is close to the Father's heart, who has made him known' (John 1.18). It defines Jesus as 'full of grace and truth' (John 1.14), a transposition into Greek of that 'abounding in steadfast love and faithfulness' (Exod. 34.6) that we saw was part of God's name. It is a very clear way of expressing that Jesus has fully assumed the name revealed to Moses and has done so in his human life. In his life of love to the very end (cf. John 13.1), he was always merciful and compassionate (cf. John 8.1–11); he was the 'Lamb of God who takes away the sin of the world' (John 1.29). And in Jesus who dies on the cross, God reveals himself as omnipotent in compassion and mercy, according to Origen's bold interpretation:

> If the Saviour descended on earth, it is on account of his compassion for humankind. Indeed, he patiently bore our sufferings before enduring the cross, before assuming our flesh. In fact, had he not suffered before, he would not have come to share human life with us. First he suffered, then he came down and showed himself to us. But what is this Passion that he went through for us? The Passion of love. And the Father himself, the God of the universe – 'slow to anger, and abounding in steadfast love and faithfulness' (Exod. 34.6) – is it not true that he, too, suffers in some way? Or do you not know that when he is concerned with human affairs, he feels a human suffering? . . . God, therefore, takes upon himself our way of being, just as the Son of God takes our sufferings on himself. The Father himself is not impassive.[9]

Conclusion

Having reached the threshold of the promised land, Moses contemplates it from the height of Mount Nebo but does not enter it (Deut. 34.1–4). He has spent all his energies in fulfilling his mission, but here his work ends. He has carried out what God asked of him, and now others will bring the exodus of the children of Israel to completion. This fine rabbinic saying is true of Moses: 'It is not up to you to finish the work, but you are not free to shirk it.'[10] Moses' greatness is seen to the very end when, in his final dialogue with God, he places the good of the children of Israel before his own good.

> God said to Moses: 'If you want the prayer "let me cross over [to the land]" (Deut. 3.25) to prevail, annul the prayer "forgive this people" (Num. 14.19). If you want "forgive this people" to prevail, annul "let me cross over".' When Moses our teacher heard this, he said: 'Lord of the world, may Moses and a thousand like him perish, but may not a fingernail of even one Israelite perish.'[11]

The Torah ends with the account of Moses' death.

> Then Moses, the servant of the LORD, died there in the land of Moab, at the LORD's command. He was buried in a valley in the land of Moab, opposite Beth-peor, but no one knows his burial place to this day. Moses was one hundred and twenty years old when he died; his sight was unimpaired and his vigour had not abated . . . Never since has there arisen a prophet in Israel like Moses, whom the LORD knew face to face. He was unequalled for all the signs and wonders that the LORD sent him to perform in the land of Egypt . . . and for all the mighty deeds and all the terrifying displays of power that Moses performed in the sight of all Israel.
>
> (Deut. 34.5–7, 10–11)

'Al pi YHWH (Deut. 34.5): this expression, normally translated 'at the LORD's command', literally means 'on the LORD's mouth'. In this way, Hebrew tradition understood that the Lord took Moses' breath away with a kiss, an extreme gesture of love towards his servant. In the end, the Lord takes care to bury Moses[12] in a place unknown to human beings. God buries Moses himself, which is the same as saying that Moses lives for ever in God, enfolded in his eternal embrace. This is why Moses will appear alive at the Transfiguration of Jesus, together with Elijah (Mark 9.2–8 and parallels).

5

Elijah and the still small voice

If in the cave in which Moses and Elijah dwelt there were an opening as big as the eye of a needle, they would not have stayed alive when the Lord passed, because it is written: 'no one shall see me and live' (Exod. 33.20).   (*b. Megillah* 19b)

'The living God', cried the people in chorus on the evening of the scene at Mount Carmel, 'is the God of the word and the answer.' But now, in the evening of the scene on Mount Horeb, the prophet Elijah in his solitude knows that the living God is the God of silence and hiddenness.

(André Neher, *The Exile of the Word*)

Lord, you are invisible in the secret of your eternity, silent in the intimacy of your love; to listen to you it is necessary to keep silent.   (*Daily Prayer of Bose*)

Introduction

From chapter 17 of the first book of Kings to chapter 2 of the second book of Kings, we find the story of Elijah, the great prophet who exercised his ministry in the kingdom of Israel, the northern kingdom, in the middle of the ninth century BC.[1] The name of this prophet is *Eliyahu*, which means 'my God is YHWH'. *Nomen omen*: in this name there is already an indication of the prophet's profound destiny, his mission to proclaim to the people of Israel that the Lord is the true God. In consequence, he will exhort them to repudiate other gods. These are the false idols whose cult had been introduced to the northern kingdom by Jezebel, the wicked

54

wife of Ahab, the king who 'did evil in the sight of the LORD more than all who were before him' (1 Kings 16.30).

Elijah is an extraordinary figure. He is the prophet par excellence of the entire Old Testament, the only one capable of representing, in his person and in his ministry, all prophecy, just as Moses sums up the law in himself. This is the testimony of the conclusion of the book of Malachi, which brings Old Testament prophecy to a close. It is a kind of appendix that places these two great figures next to each other.

Remember the teaching of my servant Moses, the statutes and ordinances that I commanded him at Horeb for all Israel.

Lo, I will send you the prophet Elijah before the great and terrible day of the LORD comes. He will turn the hearts of parents to their children and the hearts of children to their parents, so that I will not come and strike the land with a curse.   (Mal. 4.4–6)

In God's plan, Elijah – mysteriously caught up into heaven by God (cf. 2 Kings 2.11) like Enoch (cf. Gen. 5.24) – will return at the end of time as precursor, in order to carry out a work of conversion before the day of the Lord. In Jesus' time, the expectation of Elijah's return was great, so much so that Jesus himself is thought to be Elijah *redivivus* (Mark 6.15; Luke 9.8; Mark 8.28 and parallels). The Gospel passage which speaks most eloquently of Elijah is certainly that of Jesus' Transfiguration (Mark 9.2–8 and parallels). In it, Elijah and Moses are described as living and participating in God's glory; they appear at Jesus' side in the light, to speak with him 'of his departure, which he was about to accomplish at Jerusalem' (Luke 9.31), that is, about his Passion, death and resurrection. The Lord Jesus becomes glorious when the whole of Scripture converses with him, and when the Torah and the prophets point to him and reveal him. In the New Testament, however, it is above all John the Baptist, the Forerunner of the 'end time' that has begun on earth with Jesus, who impersonates Elijah. From the moment when the angel announces his birth, it is said of John that 'with the spirit and power of Elijah he will go before him' (Luke 1.17). Jesus will say that John 'is Elijah who is to come'

(Matt. 11.14), or, rather, who has already come without being recognized (cf. Mark 9.11–13), so that his coming is postponed to the end of time: 'Elijah is indeed coming and will restore all things' (Matt. 17.11). So, in obedience to this word of Jesus, Christians are still awaiting Elijah, as are the Jews, who every year during the celebration of the Passover Seder leave an empty chair for his return.

To recall Elijah's story arouses enthusiasm. Our hearts burn as we read the story of this 'prophet like fire', according to the description of him by Sirach (Ecclus. 48.1, 3, 9). At the end of the eulogy of Elijah, the author of this book even speaks of a beatitude: 'Happy are those who saw you and were adorned with your love' (Ecclus. 48.11). Elijah was truly a great sign of God, a word of God in history, and to see him meant participating in God's fire. For all of us, however, there is the possibility of contemplating Elijah with the eyes of faith. Whoever dies in love will be able to see Elijah in action on the day of the Lord.

From the Wadi Cherith to Mount Carmel

In chapter 17 of the first book of Kings, Elijah suddenly appears. Elijah the Tishbite, one of the inhabitants of Gilead, says to King Ahab: 'As the LORD the God of Israel lives, before whom I stand, there shall be neither dew nor rain these years, except by my word' (1 Kings 17.1). This man claims an extraordinary authority and an unspeakable power: in the Lord's name he shuts the heavens! We know nothing of his past, his family or his trade. His eruption into history is sudden, like the outbreak of fire, and as he came, so will he go, ascending into heaven in a fiery chariot (2 Kings 2.11). James in his Letter even feels the need to recall that he was a human like us and that his power lay in his prayer. He prayed fervently that it might not rain, and for three years and six months it did not rain on the earth. Then he prayed again, and the heaven gave rain (Jas. 5.17–18).

In the light of Elijah's subsequent prophetic preaching, we could understand this famine as being closely related to the situation of social injustice caused by idolatry. When people make their own god and refuse to see those who are in need, making a desert of human relations, they inevitably end up succumbing to the desert as it advances to destroy them too. After Elijah's abrupt entrance onto the stage,

> the word of the LORD came to him, saying, 'Go from here and turn eastwards, and hide yourself by the Wadi Cherith, which is east of the Jordan. You shall drink from the wadi, and I have commanded the ravens to feed you there.'
>
> (1 Kings 17.2–4)

'Go from here!' (*Lekh*): this is the same word as that addressed by God to Abraham at the beginning of salvation history (Gen. 12.1), the strict command to abandon the security of his own past. Here, however, there is an element that at first sight leaves one perplexed. Abraham went towards the promised land, while Elijah is already in the land and God asks him to go away from it, in view of the threat that hangs over his head from the king and queen, who regard him as 'troubler of Israel' (1 Kings 18.17). The prophet carries out his command with prompt obedience and, in the desert, experiences that God is near, as he had been during Israel's exodus from Egypt (Exod. 16.8, 12; 17.6). While he is in hiding, 'the ravens brought him bread and meat in the morning, and bread and meat in the evening' (1 Kings 17.6). It should be noted that in Hebrew the word for 'ravens' contains the same consonants as the word for 'Arabs' (cf. *Genesis Rabbah* 33.5). The prophet will be sustained by unclean animals or by pagan people, to indicate that, in each case, his condition is that of a man opposed by his people, while pagans, those outside, listen to him. And when Jesus will say that 'no prophet is accepted in the prophet's home town', he will cite the example of none other than the prophet Elijah, who was shown hospitality by a pagan widow (Luke 4.14–26).

This is Elijah, obedient and listening to God's word, the solitary figure in the desert who will appear as the forefather of monks and nuns.[2] However, he frequently makes forays into pagan lands and, for example, goes to the house of a widow living in Zarephath in

Sidon (1 Kings 17.7–24), the territory from which his enemy Jezebel comes. This woman feeds him, sharing with him her few goods, and Elijah works for her the miracle of bringing her son back to life. At the moment of leaving him, the woman cannot but say to Elijah: 'Now I know that you are a man of God, and that the word of the LORD in your mouth is truth' (1 Kings 17.24), recognizing in this way his status as prophet. Very soon, however, comes the hour of Elijah's confrontation with his persecutor, King Ahab, and, in particular, with the prophets of Baal who are in his service. The episode is well known. Ahab called together 450 prophets on Mount Carmel and Elijah, alone, challenges them all in the presence of the people.

> Elijah then came near to all the people, and said, 'How long will you go limping with two different opinions? If the LORD is God, follow him; but if Baal, then follow him.' The people did not answer him a word ... 'Let two bulls be given to us; let them choose one bull for themselves, cut it in pieces, and lay it on the wood, but put no fire to it; I will prepare the other bull and lay it on the wood, but put no fire to it. Then you call on the name of your god and I will call on the name of the LORD; the god who answers by fire is indeed God.' All the people answered, 'Well spoken!'   (1 Kings 18.21, 23–24)

The prophets call on Baal's name 'but there was no voice, and no answer' (1 Kings 18.26). Then they cry more loudly, cut their bodies and become delirious, seeking desperately to become ecstatic, but the result is even more disappointing: 'there was no voice, no answer, and no response' (1 Kings 18.29). No dialogue is possible with deaf, dumb and blind idols, fashioned by the hands of men, who, in adoring them, risk becoming immobile like them (cf. Ps. 115.5–8). Elijah makes fun of his adversaries, and even orders water to be poured on his pile of wood, then calls with all his might on the Lord, the God of Israel.

> O LORD, God of Abraham, Isaac, and Israel, let it be known this day that you are God in Israel, that I am your servant,

and that I have done all these things at your bidding. Answer
me, O LORD, answer me, so that this people may know
that you, O LORD, are God, and that you have turned their
hearts back.   (1 Kings 18.36–37)

Elijah is answered immediately and superabundantly. 'Then the
fire of the LORD fell and consumed the burnt-offering, the wood,
the stones, and the dust, and even licked up the water that was
in the trench' (1 Kings 18.38). In other words, God responds and
affirms his Presence, and so all the people prostrate themselves
to the ground and confess him as God and Lord. The story ends,
however, on a horrendously discordant note: as Moses had done
earlier (Exod. 32.25–29), *without God having commanded anything*,
Elijah assumes the terrible responsibility of a useless massacre. With
his own hands he slaughters all Baal's prophets (1 Kings 18.40).
Abusing one's power in the name of God has resulted and sometimes still results in massacres of this magnitude.

The tragic challenge is followed by the return of the long-awaited
rain (1 Kings 18.41–46). If the story ended here, the portrait of Elijah
would be triumphant. He is a man of great authority who draws
power from prayer. He is a man who appears and disappears with
incredible speed (cf. 1 Kings 18.12, 46), all the while standing firmly
in God's presence (1 Kings 17.1; 18.15). He is a man who emerges
as the winner in the encounter with idolatry, enabling him to cry:
'*Vivit Dominus!* The LORD lives!' (1 Kings 17.1, 12; 18.15). He is,
however, also a man against whom Jezebel issues a death sentence.
It is in this context that the passage of Elijah's encounter with God
is situated, 'the story that constitutes the fire of fire'.[3]

The silent God

Elijah seeks death

Ahab told Jezebel all that Elijah had done, and how he had
killed all the prophets with the sword. Then Jezebel sent a
messenger to Elijah, saying, 'So may the gods do to me, and

more also, if I do not make your life like the life of one of them by this time tomorrow.' Then he was afraid; he got up and fled for his life, and came to Beer-sheba, which belongs to Judah; he left his servant there.

But he himself went a day's journey into the wilderness, and came and sat down under a solitary broom tree. He asked that he might die: 'It is enough; now, O LORD, take away my life, for I am no better than my ancestors.' Then he lay down under the broom tree and fell asleep. Suddenly an angel touched him and said to him, 'Get up and eat.' He looked, and there at his head was a cake baked on hot stones, and a jar of water. He ate and drank, and lay down again. The angel of the LORD came a second time, touched him, and said, 'Get up and eat, otherwise the journey will be too much for you.' He got up, and ate and drank; then he went in the strength of that food for forty days and forty nights to Horeb the mount of God. (1 Kings 19.1–8)

After his portentous victory over the prophets of Baal, Elijah might seem to have been at the pinnacle of success. But now there appears on the horizon an unexpected experience, an unforeseen situation. Elijah is afraid, he feels anguish, he flees; he touches rock bottom, an experience that believers in God are not spared. Those who know God, and have received the gift of understanding his greatness, can also know hell, the abyss of his absence. Those who know the breadth of God's merciful action can also experience the prison into which even God cannot enter. All this lies behind the expression: 'he was afraid . . . and fled for his life', or 'towards his being' (*el naphsho*: 1 Kings 19.3), according to André Chouraqui's translation. It is a journey towards the knowledge of one's own depths, which takes the external form of a flight towards the south, towards Beer-sheba, on the edge of the Sinai desert. First Elijah's journey was the opposite of Abraham's, and now it is the opposite of that of the children of Israel in their exodus from Egypt.

The prophet experiences despair and, even more than fear of Jezebel, he is assailed by an unspeakable desolation, a feeling that leads him to desire death. Because of this he goes alone into the desert, leaving his servant behind; he remains without water, the only real essential in the desert, and actually thinks of suicide, of death by dehydration. He walks for a whole day and then sits down under a juniper bush, the only shrub that grows in the arid steppe. After having spent all his energy in fighting against idolatry, Elijah breaks down; his whole life seems a dismal failure.

What has happened to him? What has brought on this state of depression? Where has the man of Mount Carmel gone? Moses, too, had known frustration, had complained to God of the difficulty of leading a rebellious people and had reached the point of wanting to die (cf. Num. 11.14–15), but Elijah's situation is much darker and more obscure.

His experience is one of confusion, which we have already discussed with regard to Abraham. It is the state of utter desolation experienced by someone who no longer understands God's actions, the utter desolation of someone who has lost the capacity to give order and meaning to his own existence. In the Bible, only Psalm 88 attempts to understand this situation, but it enters into it through prayer. Here, instead, there is only the desire to have done with it, expressed through the only words that Elijah has the strength to say: 'It is enough; now, O LORD, take away my life, for I am no better than my ancestors' (1 Kings 19.4). Normally ancestors – Abraham, Isaac and Jacob – are evoked as consolation and protection and remembered in order to testify to God's faithfulness shown through them. Here, instead, Elijah associates them with a sense of common sinfulness.

Elijah, I repeat, contemplates suicide because his life seems unbearable to him, because he has lost the ability to make sense of his own existence. In him, as in every human being, there are suicidal forces at work, which cannot be ignored or removed. And they come to the surface at a time when everyone considers Elijah a victor, whereas he knows himself to be more defeated than ever.

Even the massacre of the prophets of Baal now appears to him not to have resolved anything, and thus he sees the failure of his zeal and enthusiasm for God's cause. He understands that it is illusory to think of destroying idolaters. He understands for himself what Jesus will teach when he says it is not necessary to pull up weeds, but rather one should let them grow with the grain until the Day of Judgement (cf. Matt. 13.24–30).

Elijah lies down under the juniper and hopes that death will take him as he sleeps, as earlier Hagar had done with the child Ishmael in the same place in which he is now (cf. Gen. 21.14–21). However, in this case, too, God intervenes through an angel, his messenger, who touches him and says: 'Get up and eat' (1 Kings 19.5). Elijah experiences the nearness of God, who offers him life-giving food, as happened at the beginning of his ministry by the Wadi Cherith. 'He looked, and there at his head was a cake baked on hot stones, and a jar of water' (1 Kings 19.6). Then he goes back to sleep, but again the Lord's messenger draws close to him and tells him: 'Get up and eat, otherwise the journey will be too much for you' (1 Kings 19.7). Elijah, who thought himself finished and longed for death, must begin anew in a different way; he must recommence his journey along a road indicated by the Lord, a road that is too long to be undertaken in his own strength. And so, nourished by that food, received through God's grace, Elijah walked 'forty days and forty nights to Horeb the mount of God' (1 Kings 19.8), that is, Sinai.[4] He follows the way of the exodus, repeating in his own person Israel's 40 years in the desert (Exod. 16.35; Deut. 8.2–4) and especially the 40 days of fasting with which Moses prepared himself for the meeting with God on Horeb-Sinai (Exod. 24.18; 34.28; Deut. 9.9–18). Indeed, Elijah is more and more assimilated to Moses, a second Moses for some, an anti-Moses for others.[5] In my view, he is, more simply, the Moses of silence.

Qol demamà daqqà

[On Mount Horeb Elijah] came to a cave, and spent the night there.

Then the word of the LORD came to him, saying, 'What are you doing here, Elijah?' He answered, 'I have been very zealous for the LORD, the God of hosts; for the Israelites have forsaken your covenant, thrown down your altars, and killed your prophets with the sword. I alone am left, and they are seeking my life, to take it away.'

He said, 'Go out and stand on the mountain before the LORD, for the LORD is about to pass by.' Now there was a great wind, so strong that it was splitting mountains and breaking rocks in pieces before the LORD, but the LORD was not in the wind; and after the wind an earthquake, but the LORD was not in the earthquake; and after the earthquake a fire, but the LORD was not in the fire; and after the fire a sound of sheer silence. When Elijah heard it, he wrapped his face in his mantle and went out and stood at the entrance of the cave. (1 Kings 19.9–13)

Elijah reaches Mount Horeb-Sinai, returning to the place where God revealed himself to Moses, when he gave him his holy name; it is a return to the sources of the covenant. 'He came to a cave, and spent the night there' (1 Kings 19.9). According to the rabbinic tradition, it is the same cave in which Moses had been covered by God's hand when the Lord passed before him (Exod. 33.21–23).[6] Everything, therefore, is ready for a new meeting between God and his servant. And so the Lord visits Elijah: 'What are you doing here, Elijah?' (1 Kings 19.9). 'Why are you here?' This is the profound question that God addresses to every human being, from the time of the garden of Eden. He calls us to put ourselves consciously in his presence: 'The LORD God called to the man, and said to him, "Where are you?"' (Gen. 3.9). Yet our hardness of heart tempts us to invert the question into another one: 'Where is God?' Elijah expresses his state of mind without hesitation, confessing to God: 'I have been very zealous for the LORD, the God of hosts; for the Israelites have forsaken your covenant . . . I alone am left, and they are seeking my life, to take it away' (1 Kings 19.10). In this way, he shows his confusion, admitting that his burning zeal for the Lord has, so to speak, missed the mark. His ministry, including the massacre of the prophets of Baal, seems to have ended in failure, since idolatry continues and his own life is in danger.

At this point, though very lovingly, God gives Elijah a lesson that he will never forget. He does this through an encounter narrated in four phases, or rather, in three phases plus one – the decisive one, according to a literary pattern typical of the Old Testament (cf. Amos 1—2). Elijah is ordered to go out of the cave and stand in the Lord's presence as he is about to pass by (1 Kings 19.11). The ineffable passage of the Lord is described with recourse to three natural phenomena: wind, earthquake and fire. They are the same phenomena that accompany the revelation of the Decalogue to Moses (Exod. 19.16–18), as well as the gift of the Holy Spirit on the day of Pentecost (Acts 2.2–6; see also 4.31). The elements of the Sinai theophany are renewed, but this time 'the LORD was not in [them]' (1 Kings 19.11–12). What does this mean? It is not easy to answer. The God of Israel veils the God of Moses perhaps? Or is it a case of trying to describe in a coded way the interior phenomena that characterize spiritual experience? There are countless commentaries on this passage; I would like to mention only the suggestive interpretation given by the *Midrash Tanhuma*.

> The Holy One, blessèd be he, said to Elijah: 'Man must pass through four worlds. "A strong, rushing wind" represents this world, similar to a wind that passes. "An earthquake" is the day of death, which shakes man's whole body and makes it tremble. "A fire" is the tribunal of Gehenna. "The voice of sheer silence" is the day of the great final judgement . . . On that day, there will be no one but God, as it is written: "The LORD alone will be exalted on that day" (Isa. 2.11).'[7]

Personally, having meditated long on this passage, I consider the following explanation plausible. This encounter between Elijah and God gives indications on how to proceed in the very delicate process of spiritual discernment. In particular, the first three phenomena correspond to as many risks of illusion and false inspiration in the moment of discernment, especially when it occurs in a time of crisis, like that experienced by Elijah.

The rushing wind corresponds to the interior experience of will-power, characteristic of those who appear firm as mountains, able to face every situation with their will. Their firmness is the experience of upright people who always want to be without sin. Well then, when these people reach a crisis, they understand that God is not present in human strength. In other words, only when one is broken by the events of life, can one come, by grace, to understand Paul's scandalous words: 'We had received the sentence of death so that we would rely not on ourselves but on God who raises the dead . . . Whenever I am weak, then I am strong' (2 Cor. 1.9; 12.10).

The earthquake denotes sensitivity to the things of God: the emotions aroused in us by the liturgy, the feelings that accompany meditation on Scripture, the disposition to exercise the 'spiritual senses'. These are gifts that should not be denied or removed, but there is need of great vigilance so as not to fall into the error of exercising discernment only on the basis of our senses. The risk is that of making what disturbs or moves us determine our actions. The fire represents passion, zeal and jealousy for God. It is the typical attitude of those whom I like to define as 'militant': those who, like James and John, would like to have fire descend from heaven on those who do not receive Jesus (Luke 9.54). It is the fire that drove Elijah to carry out the massacre of the pro-phets of Baal and will animate him again towards the end of his mission (cf. 2 Kings 1.10–12). It is not possible to decide when one is prey to this blinding passion, which often takes the form of wrath.

Will-power, sensitivity and zeal can be good experiences and should not be decried in themselves, but we should be on our guard against using them for discernment. God is not found in them. The text goes on to the fourth phenomenon, the one to which the whole story has been leading up: 'after the fire' there was 'a sound of sheer silence' (1 Kings 19.12).[8] It is an apparent contradiction in terms: does it mean a voice or silence? A voice of silence, naturally, is a kind of *coincidentia oppositorum* that contains a most important message: to listen to God's voice, silence and calm are required; it is necessary to quieten interior noise. It is not easy to acquire that quality of silence and listening that can allow one to catch God's silent and elusive voice (cf. Isa. 45.15), which always speaks in secret and in peace. For this reason too perhaps, with great subtlety the text leaves the reader in suspense, without affirming explicitly that God was in that voice of silence. The result of listening is never fully guaranteed.

When he heard it, Elijah covered his face with his mantle (cf. Exod. 3.16), an instinctive gesture that attests to his awareness of being once again in the Lord's presence. 'Then there came a voice to him that said, "What are you doing here, Elijah?"' (1 Kings 19.13). This is the question Elijah was already asked a little earlier, and he answers in the same way:

> I have been very zealous for the LORD, the God of hosts; for
> the Israelites have forsaken your covenant, thrown down your
> altars, and killed your prophets with the sword. I alone am
> left, and they are seeking my life, to take it away.
>
> (I Kings 19.14)

This time, however, the Lord corrects Elijah, showing him that he is not alone, as he proudly thinks. God, indeed, has saved for himself 7,000 people who have not succumbed to idolatry. More importantly, however, Elijah has to anoint Elisha as the prophet who will continue his work (1 Kings 19.15–18). Elijah can thus continue his journey, renewed in his knowledge of God, having understood that 'God's powerful voice heard on Carmel, as once by Moses on Sinai, cannot be fully understood without listening to another voice of God, the voice of silence'.[9] And when he considers the time right, God himself will put an end to his earthly life.

Conclusion

Elijah's decisive encounter with God teaches us that every day it is necessary to exercise the ears of the heart, so that the 'heart of stone' (Ezek. 11.19; 36.26) might become an understanding heart (cf. 1 Kings 3.9), which only the Lord can give. Was it not the Lord himself who could be heard walking in the garden (cf. Gen. 3.8) at the beginning? And doesn't Moses reinterpret the Sinai revelation when he says: 'You heard the sound of words but saw no form; there was only a voice' (Deut. 4.12)? When he reveals his ineffable name, God reminds people that they will never be able to possess it, they will never be able to know it fully and definitively. Gregory the Great understood this well when he wrote:

> Since we are incapable of expressing ourselves through an adequate vocabulary, limited as we are by our human weakness, we speak to God in stammers, like little children. When, however, we attain a certain knowledge of what is eternal, there occurs something that happened when, in Scripture, the great prophet Elijah was initiated into the knowledge of God. The Lord promises to pass before him, and the text then says: 'after the fire there was a murmur of a slight breeze' (cf. 1 Kings 19.12). We perceive something like the murmur of a slight breeze when, all of a sudden, in our contemplation we experience the sweet taste of infinite Truth. Only then do we truly know something of God when we realize that we can never fully know something about him.[10]

God remains an abyss of silence, a silence that is subtle and restrained, inhabited by that Word who is the source of life and daily nourishment on the way to the kingdom, where we shall see him 'face to face' (1 Cor. 13.12), beyond the embrace of death. Indeed, God is truly both speech and silence, not a deaf and dumb silence, but a silence that is communication other than by words, a language that in certain situations can show itself to be more efficacious and eloquent than any speech.

In a liturgical text of the Qumran community, the *Songs of the Sabbath Sacrifice*, the expression 'voice of silence' recurs more than once to designate the angelic liturgy that accompanies the earthly one.

> The cherubim prostrate themselves before God and bless him. When they rise, the silent voice of God is heard and there is rejoicing when their wings are raised: the voice of the silence of God . . . God's silent voice is heard in their movement as they bless and praise the Holy One . . . The voice of joyful jubilation falls silent and there is silence as all the celestial beings bless God.[11]

We ought to recall this text when, at the heart of the eucharistic liturgy, we sing the Sanctus, the acclamation that, with all the invisible creation and the saints of heaven, celebrates the holiness of God and at the same time proclaims his coming among us in the past, present and future (cf. Rev. 4.8): 'Holy, holy, holy, Lord God of hosts. Heaven and earth are full of your glory [cf. Isa. 6.3]. Hosanna in the highest.' Indeed, God is the thrice Holy One, the thrice Other, yet he always desires to communicate his Presence to human beings, asking only that his 'voice of sheer silence' be received. When believers blame God for being mute, when we attribute to him the emptiness of our own heart, this is in fact due to our inability to listen, because we seek from him a word that is in our own image and likeness.

6

The vocation of Isaiah

Holy in the highest heavens, the dwelling of his Presence, holy over the earth, the work of his power, holy for ages of ages is the Lord of the universe.

(*Targum of Jonathan* on Isa. 6.3)

You are holy and your name is holy and the holy [angels] praise you every day. We sanctify your name in the world, as it is sanctified in the highest, as it is written by your prophet: 'And one called to another and said: "Holy, holy, holy is the LORD of hosts; the whole earth is full of his glory" (Isa. 6.3).'

(From the synagogue blessing *El qadosh* (Holy God))

What good is it to you that the 'earth is full of his glory' (Isa. 6.3), if you do not partake of this 'fullness of God' (Eph. 3.19)? . . . And how is the fullness of God's glory realized for each one of us? If what I do and say is for the glory of God, my acts are full of this glory. If '[my] going out and [my] coming in' (Ps. 121.8), 'my food, my drink, all that I do is for the glory of God' (cf. 1 Cor. 10.31), I too participate in this word: 'the whole earth is full of his glory' (Isa. 6.3).

(Origen, *Homilies on Isaiah* 4.2)

Introduction

In the Old Testament apocryphal text entitled *The Ascension of Isaiah*, it is recounted that during the reign of the wicked Manasseh (687–642 BC), Isaiah fled into the desert with his community of prophets following the persecution unleashed by the king against him. Then Bekhirah, a false prophet, addressed Manasseh in these words:

> Isaiah and his companions prophesy concerning Jerusalem and concerning the cities of Judah and Benjamin, saying that they will be led into slavery by you, my Lord the King, and that you will end up in chains in a cage for wild animals. Now, they tell lies . . . Isaiah personally has said: 'I am a visionary superior to the prophet Moses.' In fact, Moses has said: 'no one shall see [God] and live' (Exod. 33.20), but Isaiah has said: 'my eyes have seen the King, the LORD of hosts!' (Isa. 6.5) Know, then, O King, that he is a liar.[1]

As a result of these accusations, Isaiah was arrested and died a martyr – like all the prophets, according to Jewish tradition – sawn in two by his persecutors while speaking words inspired by the Holy Spirit.[2]

Now, this vision narrated by the prophet seems, at first reading, to contradict the biblical saying that no one can see God and remain alive. In reality, however, for Isaiah, as for Moses and for every other figure of Scripture, it remains impossible to see God directly, face to face: here on earth we can see God only with the eyes of faith, because 'we walk by faith, not by sight' (2 Cor. 5.7). Nevertheless, the affirmation of Isaiah retains great force: 'my eyes have seen the King, the LORD of hosts' (Isa. 6.5), an affirmation that needs careful unpacking. It is a matter of discerning how God makes himself present in an ever new, specific and very personal way in the life of those who believe in him and seek him.

We are at chapter 6 of the book of Isaiah,[3] a kind of introduction to the so-called 'book of Emmanuel', God-with-us (Isa. 6.1—12.6), and the prophet gives an account of his own calling. Unlike the more usual practice in prophetic literature (Jer. 1; Ezek. 1 etc.), the story of his vocation is not placed at the beginning of the book. This was probably to emphasize the fact that Isaiah elaborated on his calling many times, making of it an intuitive and visual synthesis of all the major themes of his preaching, in which judgement and salvation appear to be inseparable. In this passage, moreover, we have an account of a theophany, striking for its symbolic and figurative language, anticipating the apocalyptic. However, it is not necessary to interpret this account as if Isaiah were speaking of a transcendental, mystical experience, a vision that corresponds exactly to what is being described. No, we have here an experience of pure faith,[4] which in itself is impossible to describe. Yet Isaiah tries to speak of what cannot be expressed, conscious of how difficult it is to describe his encounter with God. On the other hand, the experience of Isaiah 6 is not disembodied; it is a revelation, a raising of the veil of history by God, to such an extent that Martin Buber understood it as a 'theo-political vision'.[5] It is not by chance that the prophet presents the Lord as having the appearance of an Eastern king of his time. He had seen or heard tell of the great king of Assyria splendidly robed and surrounded by a court of councillors, but just when Assyria is advancing threateningly towards the borders of Israel, Isaiah affirms that the true King is the Lord. 'My eyes have seen the King, the LORD of hosts' (Isa. 6.5).

Indeed, the God of Israel acts in history, and the prophet sent by him stands in history, in full solidarity with the people as they turn to God. At the same time, he stands on God's side, to convert the people through his preaching.

'*I saw the Lord sitting on a throne, high and lofty*'

In the year that King Uzziah died, I saw the Lord sitting on a throne, high and lofty; and the hem of his robe filled the temple. Seraphs were in attendance above him; each had six wings: with two they covered their faces, and with two they covered their feet, and with two they flew. And one called to another and said: 'Holy, holy, holy is the LORD of hosts; the whole earth is full of his glory.'

The pivots on the thresholds shook at the voices of those who called, and the house filled with smoke. (Isa. 6.1–4)

We are in the middle of the eighth century BC, more precisely in 740–739, when Uzziah, the anointed king, descendant of David, died after the terrible sickness of leprosy had kept him segregated from the worship of the community in the Temple. He had in fact challenged God's holiness and violated his glory by daring to enter the sanctuary to offer incense, which was the priests' prerogative (2 Chron. 26.16–21). For this he had been struck by leprosy and had ended his days in shameful impurity.

In that year, Isaiah enters the Temple of Jerusalem, the place in which the Lord dwells (cf. 1 Kings 8.10–13), and it is here that he has an encounter with God that will change his life for ever. Isaiah is in the vestibule, in the *ulam*, and before him stands the *debir*, the holy of holies, the place of God's Shekhinah; between the prophet and the holy of holies is the altar of incense on which are burned spices in the Lord's honour. The prophet knows that the holy of holies contains the ark of the covenant, the throne of the Lord God of the universe, and that over it stand two cherubim in adoration, protecting it with their great wings (cf. 1 Kings 8.6–7).

In short, he is in adoration of the one true and living God; he stands before God's face (cf. Ps. 16.11 etc.) in fear.

And then he has an ineffable experience. 'I saw the Lord sitting on a throne, high and lofty; and the hem of his robe filled the temple' (Isa. 6.1). The Lord is perceived by Isaiah in his kingly transcendence. He stands above, in a raised place, in a position of dominion, and is wrapped in a robe that descends to cover the whole floor of the Temple. It should be noted that the prophet says he saw the Lord but then does not describe his appearance in concrete terms; he limits himself instead to describing the attributes of his power. Around the Lord who is seated on the throne stand the flaming creatures, the Seraphim (a term derived from the root *saraf*, 'to burn'). They are creatures of fire, mentioned only here in all of Scripture. They remain suspended in the air and fly continually. 'Each had six wings: with two they covered their faces, and with two they covered their feet [a euphemism for the genitals], and with two they flew' (Isa. 6.2). In that whirlwind of fire the Seraphim call to one another: 'Holy, holy, holy is the LORD of hosts;[6] the whole earth is full of his glory' (Isa. 6.3). It is the proclamation of God's name as King and Lord of the whole earth but also the proclamation of his holiness: *qadosh*, 'holy'. This is God's quintessential attribute; in the book of Isaiah it occurs 37 times (as compared, for example, with only twice each in Jeremiah and Ezekiel). Holiness is distinction, separation, otherness. The Lord God is holy, distinct and separate: thrice other, that is, holy in the highest degree, most holy. God's holiness indicates a power that shines and consumes, hence is possessed of a glory (*kavod*), a burden that imposes itself and fills the whole earth. Holiness is the essence of God's glory, and glory is the manifestation of his holiness.

At that song, the Temple shakes, the doorposts vibrate and the smoke that rises from the altar of incense fills the whole Temple (Isa. 6.4). The smoke of the Cloud, the Shekhinah of God, fills the Temple as on the day of its dedication by Solomon (1 Kings 8.10–12). Indeed, Isaiah's vision is nourished by the liturgy, showing how it is an eminent means by which the Lord comes to believers. How can we forget that this hymn to God's holiness, paraphrased in Psalm 99.3, 5, 9, had found an important place in Jewish liturgy,[7] and then, after recurring in Revelation 4.8 ('Holy, holy, holy, the Lord God the Almighty, who was and is and is to come'), has been reworked to assume the form of the Trisagion or Sanctus, the acclamation placed at the heart of the eucharistic celebration by all the Christian churches?[8]

'Woe is me! I am lost ...'

And I said: 'Woe is me! I am lost,[9] for I am a man of unclean lips, and I live among a people of unclean lips; yet my eyes have seen the King, the LORD of hosts!'

Then one of the seraphs flew to me, holding a live coal that had been taken from the altar with a pair of tongs. The

seraph touched my mouth with it and said: 'Now that this
has touched your lips, your guilt has departed and your sin
is blotted out.'   (Isa. 6.5–7)

Faced with this vision, the prophet is struck with terror, fear caused
by an awareness of his own unworthiness; he perceives that God's
holiness is unbearable for a human being. 'Woe is me! I am lost'
(Isa. 6.5), he exclaims, just as, confronted by the holiness of Jesus
Christ, Peter will say: 'Go away from me, Lord, for I am a sinful man!'
(Luke 5.8). 'I am a man of unclean lips, and I live among a people
of unclean lips.' The prophet's greatness lies in his ability to live
in full solidarity with his people, without feeling himself to be
more righteous or better than his neighbours.

Isaiah is aware that his sin and his guilt make communion
with the holy God impossible for him. In his words we can discern
an important theological innovation. For the first time in the
Bible, the category of impure is not used to refer to a force of
nature that resembles the sacred, a force that objectively takes away
strength (cf. Gen. 31.35; 1 Sam. 21.5–7 etc.). Isaiah affirms that
what makes him impure is not something exterior but rather his
sin and transgression.[10] What makes man impure is sin and guilt;
this is the real impurity. This conception will be carried to its
logical conclusion by Jesus when he says: 'There is nothing outside
a person that by going in can defile, but the things that come out
are what defile' (Mark 7.15; cf. Matt. 15.11).

As soon as Isaiah assumes and manifests this awareness, his
conversion is effected by the Lord. One of the flaming creatures
flies towards him holding in his hands a burning coal taken from
the altar of incense and touches his mouth, saying: 'Now that
this has touched your lips, your guilt [*'awon*] has departed and
your sin [*chatta*] is blotted out' (Isa. 6.7). Isaiah has confessed his
impurity but God, through one of the Seraphim, tells him that
the very sources of impurity, guilt and sin have been destroyed.
It is the experience of a radical rebirth, in which God's holiness
is communicated to the future prophet. As the Lord's hand will

touch Jeremiah's lips (Jer. 1.9–10), as Ezekiel will receive a book
to devour (Ezek. 3.1–3), so Isaiah receives on his lips the purifying
fire. It is a terrible, burning experience, in which people discover
themselves as sinners, but at the same time feel themselves for-
given and brought into communion with God, who in holiness
overcomes their sin. Isaiah is now restored; he is a new creature,
he is finally made worthy of being God's spokesman.

'Here am I; send me!'

> Then I heard the voice of the Lord saying, 'Whom shall I
> send, and who will go for us?' And I said, 'Here am I; send
> me!' And he said, 'Go and say to this people: "Keep listening,
> but do not comprehend; keep looking, but do not under-
> stand." Make the mind of this people dull, and stop their
> ears, and shut their eyes, so that they may not look with their
> eyes, and listen with their ears, and comprehend with their
> minds, and turn and be healed.'   (Isa. 6.8–10)

'Whom shall I send, and who will go for us?' This terse question
resounds in the divine assembly to which Isaiah has been admitted,
a divine silence punctuated by the singing of the Trisagion.
To this question Isaiah responds with only two words: 'Hinneni
shelacheni,' 'Here am I; send me!' (Isa. 6.8) As we have already
seen, 'Here am I' tells of a radical readiness, a total surrender of
man to God. It is the response that God expects from those whom
he calls, from Abraham (cf. Gen. 22.1ff.) to Mary (cf. Luke 1.38).
Isaiah does not know what he is to do; he does not know the style
he is supposed to assume or the purpose of his mission, but in
complete freedom and for love of the Lord who revealed himself
to him, he says, 'Send me!' Here we have the birth of a prophet,
entirely willed, made and created by God. At the moment of his
calling, he can only respond by predisposing everything so that
the Lord's word might be fulfilled in his life, telling him, in essence:
'Here I am, here at your service.' Thus the mission that God wants

to confer on the prophet is assumed by him. Only at this point does God reveal to him the nature and the cost of the mission itself. Normally, the calling fills the individual with courage and strength, while the mission is understood in depth only later and is often a source of great suffering for the one called. In this case, the mission entrusted to Isaiah is disconcerting, even scandalous. His task will be to harden the hearts of the nation of believers, making their ears deaf, blinding their eyes and obscuring their understanding (Isa. 6.9–10). How is such a ministry possible? Why does God call Israel, not 'my people' (cf. Isa. 1.3; 3.12, 15; 5.13), but in a detached way 'this people'? Why does the sending of the prophet worsen the situation instead of improving it? Why will Isaiah's mission be a ministry of condemnation rather than salvation? These are disquieting and enigmatic questions. Is God perhaps sending the prophet to condemn the people because he wants their death and their defeat? No, the mission entrusted to Isaiah must be viewed through a spiritual lens.

First of all, in God's interventions we should always and only read the fulfilment of a plan of love, because there is no evil in God and he takes no pleasure in suffering (cf. Ps. 5.4). The Lord God is always and only 'grace/love and faithfulness' (*chesed we-emeth*: Pss. 25.10; 85.11 etc.) and when he gives his word, he does it to save humankind. He does not want us to perish but rather to be converted and live (cf. Ezek. 18.23; 33.11). The sending of Isaiah marks, so to speak, the last attempt on God's part to save Israel from impending catastrophe. Truly, the people, their kings and their priests have shown themselves constantly unfaithful to the covenant. God has continued to send prophets but all seems to be of no avail. What actually happens? The unfaithful children of Israel, hard of heart, with their ears closed and their eyes blinded by sin, instead of being converted and returning to God when he speaks through the prophets' ministry, persist in their rebellion and transgressions against the covenant and in their sin. In this way, the preaching of God's word by the prophet ends by making their hearts harder than ever. This is not God's intention, but in the relationship between God and his people, the same thing happens that often occurs on an interpersonal level. The good done to an evil person, instead of converting him or her, makes that individual still more evil.

Here lies the paradox of Isaiah's mission. God sends him to preach conversion: *teshuvah*; he sends him to call Israel to faith, but 'this people' does not listen. God's word is always efficacious (cf. Isa. 55.10–11; Heb. 4.12–13); with its power it always produces some effect. It does not leave things the same as they were before. It is not possible to be neutral or indifferent to the Word: either one is converted or the situation of sin becomes worse; *tertium non datur*. This is the way it is and it cannot be otherwise. The Word has power in itself, and when it comes to someone who refuses to accept it, the situation of that person becomes worse than before. The result of failing to listen to the Word is so serious that these verses of Isaiah will be repeated more than once in the New Testament. Jesus quotes them when he is questioned about his reason for speaking in parables (Mark 4.10–12 and parallels); the author of the Fourth Gospel and Paul use it to explain the incredulity which meets the preaching of Jesus and the Apostles (cf. John 12.39–41; Acts 28.24–27; Rom. 11.7–8).[11]

To sum up: when Isaiah asks for conversion on the part of the people, he paradoxically hardens their hearts, makes their ears deaf and blinds their eyes, ending by averting conversion and healing. Incomprehension of God's word becomes more profound and so catastrophe appears to be a necessity. When one embarks on and follows the path of evil, devastation is imminent.

'How long, O Lord?'

I said: 'How long, O Lord?' And he said: 'Until cities lie waste without inhabitant, and houses without people, and the land is utterly desolate; until the LORD sends everyone far away, and vast emptiness is in the midst of the land.

(Isa. 6.11–12)

Isaiah, who feels himself to be so at one with his people, has a terrible ministry – 'I am a man of unclean lips, and I live among a people of unclean lips' (Isa. 6.5) – he must now place himself on God's side, in the position of someone who is against his people. This is the prophet's destiny. He is forced into a constantly changing attitude: he is on God's side as he proclaims the Word and coming judgement, but when punishment appears on the horizon, he places himself on the people's side 'against' God, interceding insistently, asking for mercy, patience and forgiveness (cf. Amos 7.5: 'O Lord GOD, cease, I beg you! How can Jacob stand? He is so small!'). Here stands the true prophet: with God and with the people, against God and against the people.

Once he has heard the announcement that defines his mission, Isaiah immediately assumes the position of an intercessor: 'How long, O Lord?' (Isa. 6.11), a question that is often to be found on the psalmist's lips (cf. Pss. 6.3; 13.2 etc.). The point is, is there an end to this crisis, this situation of judgement, this night? Isaiah will ask the same question later on, 'Sentinel, what of the night?' (Isa. 21.11). The prophet feels emotion and anguish; he is deeply moved for the people to whom he is sent with a ministry of judgement.

The Lord answers him with a description of the catastrophe towards which Israel is heading: depopulated and devastated cities, abandoned houses, uncultivated fields. Here there is not yet any prophecy of the fall of Jerusalem, the holy city, but the trial will come, the judgement of the unfaithful people will take place and an hour of justice will sound for God's people. It is not God who punishes but Israel, who has freely set out on the way of death and the path of idolatry, choosing to live in unrighteousness and violence, and the outcome cannot but be devastation.

Conclusion

Even if a tenth part remains in it, it will be burned again, like a terebinth or an oak whose stump remains standing when it is felled. The holy seed is its stump.   (Isa. 6.13)

Is it the end of the history of salvation? No, and this verdict closes in great hope, expressed in a marvellous parable. Even if the people should become like a destroyed forest, of which only stumps remain, they will still be capable of sending out shoots, of generating a holy seed. The great forest is cut down, but from the stumps that remain a bud will grow, because they are a holy seed. This is the revelation of Israel's 'faithful remnant', which begins here in Isaiah and will be taken up by successive prophets; this is the revelation that will be fulfilled in the shoot that will come forth from the stump or stock of Jesse (Isa. 11.1), the Messiah, Jesus.

Crisis or *deminutio*, therefore, is not to be feared. The important thing is to be a holy stump, because only in this way will holy shoots be born, capable of making everything ready so that God's plan of salvation might be fulfilled and the Word continue its course on earth (cf. 2 Thess. 3.1). Isaiah's vocation teaches that every encounter with God should reinforce the consciousness and will of believers to be his obedient servants, whatever the cost, to be nothing but the 'servants of his Word' (cf. Luke 1.2).

7

Where is God?

———◆·◆·◆———

God . . . is not far from each one of us. For 'In him we live
and move and have our being'.   (Acts 17.27–28)

Rabbi Isaac Meir of Gher was asked: 'Where does God live?'
And he replied: 'Where doesn't he live?'
                          (Martin Buber, *Tales of the Chasidim*)

God became man so that man can become truly man.

Introduction

During his visit to Auschwitz concentration camp on 28 May 2006,
Benedict XVI cried: 'The question always arises anew: Where was
God in those days? Why was he silent? How could he tolerate this
excess of destruction, this triumph of evil?' The question, 'Where
is God?' can always be heard in man's heart. Its only answer, however, is in faith, that is, in the believer's loyalty to the God whom
no one has seen or can see as long as he or she is alive (cf. Exod.
33.20; 1 Tim. 6.16). This is a God who, as Deuteronomy reveals,
is a God who speaks (Deut. 4.32–33) and a God who loves (Deut.
7.7–8). The question concerning the 'where of God', the 'place' of
God, is the essential question of holy Scripture. It is therefore not
by chance that in Judaism God himself, on account of his unpro-
nounceable name, has been called by the circumlocution *maqom
acher*, the 'other place', or simply by the term *maqom*, 'place'.

The question about the place of God's presence occurs at
various times in the Bible, first of all on the lips of those who
affirm: 'There is no God' (Pss. 14.1; 53.1). It is also to be found
on the lips of the enemies of believers, those, that is, who mock

the faith and the firm loyalty of the righteous to their God. These last are compelled to reply to such jeers with the words of the Psalms: 'My tears have been my food day and night, while people say to me continually, "Where is your God?"' (Ps. 42.3) and, 'Why should the nations say, "Where is their God?"' (Pss. 79.10; 115.2). Significantly, the same question is found on the lips of believers in the hour of catastrophe, the hour of the triumph of evil. It is present in Third Isaiah, a prophecy that follows the *shoah* of Jerusalem in 587 BC and the deportation of the children of Israel into Babylon.

> Where is the one who brought them up out of the sea with the shepherds of his flock? Where is the one who put within them his holy spirit . . . who led them through the depths?
>
> (Isa. 63.11, 13)

In short, where is God, he who in the past had acted with his powerful arm and showed himself to be *go'el*, redeemer (cf. Isa. 41.14; 43.14; 44.6 etc.), while now he seems absent and inert?

This same question, however, can become a sin for those who have adhered to the Lord, indeed it is the great sin. It is an unbelief and lack of trust in God, a desire to put him to the test, a complacent indulgence in the questioning that faith involves. In the end believers ask themselves: in spite of having seen the wonders worked by God during the exodus: 'Is the Lord in our midst or not?' A famous passage in the book of Exodus bears witness to this:

> From the wilderness of Sin the whole congregation of the Israelites journeyed by stages, as the LORD commanded. They camped at Rephidim, but there was no water for the people to drink. The people quarrelled with Moses and said, 'Give us water to drink.' Moses said to them, 'Why do you quarrel with me? Why do you test the LORD?' . . . He called the place Massah and Meribah, because the Israelites quarrelled and tested the LORD, saying, 'Is the LORD among us or not?'
>
> (Exod. 17.1–2, 7)

Here it should be clearly stated that faith in God does not permit such a question. It does not allow incredulity to prevail over confident trust in the Lord. Instead, the question is turned around and there is a suggestion that, in the hour of evil, today as yesterday, in Auschwitz as in other places of unspeakable inhumanity, the issue should really be: 'Where was, where is man? Where was, where is our humanity?' This is the real question that believers should ask themselves; or rather, it is the same question that God addressed to Adam after the fall: 'Adam, where are you?' (cf. Gen. 3.9).

Finally, it should not be forgotten that God's presence is always elusive:[1]

> A presence that not only eludes us when we think of being in possession of it, but that always and continually takes the initiative of new departures in which man is as it were torn away from himself.[2]

After analysing the encounters between God and some of the most significant figures of the Old Testament, I would like now to take a path that is complementary to the one followed so far. I will read through sacred Scripture, placing myself in the position of listening to the word of God contained in it, so as to understand its message concerning:

- where God is to be found;
- where, in consequence, we can meet him.

Where is God, the Creator of the universe?

It is certainly not by chance that the Bible opens with the solemn and poetic account of the creation (Gen. 1.1–2, 4).[3] By his Word and his Spirit that hovered over the waters (cf. Gen. 1.2), God created light and darkness, heaven and earth, the life of all creatures, and finally, on the sixth day, he created humankind, *adam*, 'in his image and likeness' (cf. Gen. 1.26–27). So God's work of creation took place, 'God saw everything that he had made, and indeed, it was *tov me'od*, very good' (Gen. 1.31). And so, on the seventh day, after finishing his work, God 'rested [verb *shabat*] . . . from all the work that he had done' (Gen. 2.2).

In this conclusion of the creation story, not only is the origin of the *shabat* given, the Sabbath, a day of rest from all work, but we are also told that God has not expressed himself totally in creation. He has not manifested himself fully in his work, because he has distanced himself from it and transcended it. The creation is a community of creatures and as such is not God; it is not a divine reality, since God is not contained in it. Indeed, 'heaven and earth are full of [his] glory' as the liturgy sings in the Sanctus. They tell of it and bear witness to it, but are incapable of containing God, of being the place of a fulfilled encounter between God and man. It is true that 'the heavens are telling the glory of God; and the firmament proclaims his handiwork' (Ps. 19.1), and that 'ever since the creation of the world his eternal power and divine nature, invisible though they are, have been understood and seen through the things he has made' (Rom. 1.20). Nevertheless, God has reserved for himself another mode, fuller and more efficacious, for his manifestation to humankind, and the Sabbath is like a sign and prophecy of it.[4]

To express God's transcendence, Scripture more than once affirms that God is 'he who sits in the heavens' (Ps. 2.4), that 'our God is in the heavens' (Ps. 115.3), that 'the LORD's throne is in heaven'. He is indeed the Holy One, distinct and separate from his work, 'other' than the universe. The believing Jew, therefore, in confessing that God dwells in the heavens beyond creation, proclaims that he is above every visible reality, that he is, precisely, *Qadosh*, holy, or, rather, the thrice-holy (cf. Isa. 6.3). This is a vision that has become the patrimony of Christians too. Indeed, we too invoke 'Our Father in heaven' (Matt. 6.9) and with him in heaven dwells Jesus as the risen Lord (Mark 16.19; Col. 3.1), who will come with power and glory on the last day of this creation (Mark 13.26 and parallels; Phil. 3.21).

So the very truth that God has distanced himself from his works has made revelation, the raising of God's veil, necessary. He has come down from the heavens to speak to his people and to meet them, to the point of descending in the Son, the Word made flesh in Jesus of Nazareth, thus showing human beings his face. Here is how the Prologue of St John's Gospel, to which we shall return below, describes the descent of God in the Son:

> The Word became flesh and lived among us, and we have seen his glory . . . No one has ever seen God. It is God the only Son, who is close to the Father's heart, who has made him known. (John 1.14, 18)

In the meantime, let us observe more closely this revelation of God's Presence to humankind throughout history.

God reveals himself and dwells in the midst of his people

As we have seen, God began to reveal himself to humankind by calling Abraham, the first believer in the living and true God, making an everlasting covenant with him and giving him a promise and a blessing in favour of all humanity (cf. Gen. 12.1–3; 15.1–7; 17.1–8; 22.18). With the passing of time, God confirmed his covenant to the patriarchs, becoming 'the God of Abraham, the God of Isaac, and the God of Jacob' (Exod. 3.6 etc.). He then revealed himself to Moses, giving him his holy name (Exod. 3.7–15) and entrusting to him the mission of liberating Israel from the slavery of Egypt. The God who revealed himself to the patriarchs dwells in heaven, but he wanted to meet Moses in a precise place: on Mount Horeb, the mountain of God, in a burning bush (Exod. 3.1–6). And in entrusting Moses with his mission, God gave him at the same time the promise: 'when you have brought the people out of Egypt, you shall worship God on this mountain' (Exod. 3.12). This is the goal, the final end of the exodus: freedom from slavery to serve God and encounter him on Sinai.

Once the exodus from Egypt has taken place, the redeemed people meet God on Mount Sinai to enter into a covenant with him. The Lord will be their God and Israel will be his people (Lev. 26.12). It is at this point that we read:

The glory of the LORD settled [verb *shakan*] on Mount Sinai,
and the cloud[5] covered it for six days; on the seventh day he
called to Moses out of the cloud. Now the appearance of the
glory of the LORD was like a devouring fire on the top of
the mountain.   (Exod. 24.16–17)

And so the meeting between God and his people takes place,
sanctioned by the covenant concluded on the basis of the Ten
Commandments (Exod. 20.1–21; Deut. 5.1–22); it is a covenant
concluded with the blood that Moses sprinkled on God's altar and
on the people (Exod. 24.6–8), to signify the same life, a profound
communion established between God and his people.

In the Exodus text quoted above there is one expression that
will be a guiding thread: 'the glory of the LORD settled'. The *kavod
Adonai*[6] is the very being of God in its manifestation and communication, God's Glory, the luminous splendour of his Presence.
It comes to dwell – that is, to pitch its tent, which is the literal mean-
ing of the verb *shakan* – on earth, and specifically on Mount Sinai.
God chooses a precise place in space to reveal himself and enter
into relationship with humankind. For the people liberated from
Egypt, or rather, for the children of Israel who have been made a
people in covenant with God, God comes, therefore, to dwell on
Sinai. In this way, he can be God in the midst of his people, the
'Immanu-El, the God-with-us (cf. Isa. 7.14; 8.8, 10).

The people of Israel, who were called to the service and worship (*'avodah*) of God in the desert (cf. Exod. 3.12; 5.1 etc.), out
of the 'house of slavery' (Exod. 13.3, 14; 20.2; Deut. 5.6 etc.), are,
however, a people journeying towards the promised land. Thus
God, who is in covenant with them, chooses to accompany them
in their exodus. And so, by order of God, Moses constructs 'the
tent of meeting' (cf. Exod. 27.21; 28.43 etc.), which will always
follow the people in their pilgrimage to 'a land flowing with milk
and honey' (Exod. 3.8). In fact, the Lord says: 'Have them make
me a sanctuary, so that I may dwell [verb *shakan*] among them'
(Exod. 25.8).

> I will meet the Israelites there, and it shall be sanctified by
> my glory . . . I will dwell [verb *shakan*] among the Israelites,
> and I will be their God. And they shall know that I am the
> LORD their God. (Exod. 29.43, 45–46)

And at the end of the book of Exodus, we read, 'So Moses finished
the work. Then the cloud covered the tent of meeting, and the glory
of the LORD filled the tabernacle [*mishkan*]' (Exod. 40.33–34). Here
God meets with his people and in their turn the people adore and
meet God. Through Moses, they receive the word of God who is
unique among all gods, insofar as he is a God who speaks and loves.

Once the Israelites have entered the land, this tent of meeting
between God and his people will continue its own pilgrimage. At
first it will be set up by Joshua at Shiloh (Josh. 18; Judg. 18.31),
then David will bring it to Jerusalem (2 Sam. 6.17) and finally it
will have a permanent place in the Temple built by Solomon (1 Kings
8.1–9). The first book of Kings says,

> And when the priests came out of the holy place, a cloud
> filled the house of the LORD, so that the priests could not
> stand to minister because of the cloud; for the glory of the
> LORD filled the house of the LORD. Then Solomon said, 'The
> LORD has said that he would dwell [verb *shakan*] in thick
> darkness.' (1 Kings 8.10–12)

Here then, finally, is the quintessential place of God's Presence. The
God who dwells in the heavens establishes a place for his Presence on
earth, the holy of holies (cf. Exod. 26.33–34; 1 Kings 8.6 etc.) inside
the Temple – all this, let us not forget, with the aim of meeting his
people. In perfect accord with scriptural vocabulary, the Jewish tradition has called this Presence of God by the term Shekhinah,[7] a noun
derived from the verb *shakan*, which we meet often in the Bible. The
holy of holies, that room in the heart of the Temple which contained
the ark of the covenant (1 Kings 6.14–22), was truly the place of the
Presence of God in the world, the revelation of the invisible God;
it was the place in which the Hebrew God could be localized.[8]

The people's infidelity, however, and the breach of the covenant will cause the destruction of the Temple and the profanation of the holy of holies, the place of the Shekhinah. But when in 587 BC the Babylonians, led by Nebuchadnezzar, enter the Temple and loot it, according to Ezekiel's vision the Presence of God signified by the Cloud will abandon the holy of holies. It will rise towards heaven and will go to rest east of Jerusalem, on the Mount of Olives, so as to follow the column of those deported to Babylon (Ezek. 10.18–22; 11.22–25). God never abandons his people, not even when they repudiate the covenant, and his Presence always accompanies them. When the time comes for the return from Babylon, the second exodus, the Shekhinah will be at the head of the people. In the Second Temple, it will again take up its dwelling in the holy of holies (cf. Ezek. 41.3–4; 43.1–4), as a sign of God-with-us.

At the end of this journey through the pages of the Old Testament, I should point out that Ezekiel, the last of the prophets to contemplate the Lord's Glory, sees in it 'something that seemed like a human form' (Ezek. 1.26).

The Shekhinah becomes flesh in Jesus and makes his dwelling in Christians

The New Testament affirms that in the 'fullness of time' (Gal. 4.4), at the fulfilment of all the promises and covenants, in the messianic age, God visits his people (cf. Luke 1.68) in a unique and unrepeatable way. He becomes *'Immanu-El*, God-with-us, in Jesus, the Son of the Virgin Mary (cf. Matt. 1.23).

The evangelist Luke in particular establishes a parallel between the Lord's Glory, signified by the Cloud that covered the tent of meeting, and the power of the Most High that overshadows Mary (Luke 1.35), thus indicating the new site of God's Presence. Mary is identifiable as the site of the Shekhinah because in her womb she carries Jesus, God made man, the Shekhinah in the flesh.[9] In Mary, daughter of Zion and the new Eve, womb of the new humanity, the promise made by God to his people finds fulfillment. 'Lo,

I will come and dwell in your midst' (Zech. 2.10). Now it becomes clear what God's intention was in coming down to meet man and establish communion with him. It was not only to set up his dwelling in the midst of his people through the tent or the Temple (sacraments of his Presence, certainly, but seen as temporary), but rather to set up his dwelling in man, to make man his dwelling.

Jewish tradition also bears witness to this awareness. A story of the Chasidim goes like this:

> When rabbi Baruch used to come to the words of the Psalm:
> 'I will not give sleep to my eyes or slumber to my eyelids, until
> I find a place for the Lord' (Ps. 132.4–5), he would stop and
> say to himself: 'Until I find myself and make of myself a
> dwelling ready to receive the Shekhinah.'[10]

With the descent of the Shekhinah into Mary's womb, the Jerusalem Temple remains a 'house of prayer' (Mark 11.17). Significantly, according to Luke's Gospel, when Jesus is 12 years old, he will say to Mary and Joseph in the Temple: 'Did you not know that I must be in my Father's house?' (Luke 2.49). The Temple is Jesus' home: in the Acts of the Apostles the same Luke states that Jesus will appear to Paul in the Temple itself (Acts 22.17–21), showing that he has become its Lord.

However, Matthew, who also witnesses to Jesus' very special relationship with the Temple, puts these words into the Master's mouth: 'I tell you, something greater than the temple is here' (Matt. 12.6), thus giving a foretaste of what John will say explicitly, namely that Jesus is now the true temple, the definitive temple. The Temple of Jerusalem, the place of God's Presence, willed by him, will be supplanted as the place of encounter between God and humankind. Now the new and definitive place of encounter is Jesus of Nazareth. And, in Jesus, the place is human flesh.

It is the Fourth Gospel that, through a full development of the theme of Glory, brings to completion the long journey initiated by Scripture in response to the question, 'Where is God?' With a great understanding of language, in the Prologue that deals with the

Incarnation of the Logos, John writes: 'The Word became flesh and lived [*eskenosen*] among us, and we have seen his glory' (John 1.14).

Note the assonance between *shakan* and *skenóo*, the two verbs that describe the pitching of the tent, the dwelling. The evangelist's intention in making this verbal reference is clear. Humanity, the flesh of Jesus Christ, is the definitive place of God's Presence.[11] God became man; his Presence has been located in time and space in Jesus, the man in whom God has fully revealed his Glory. Jesus is the proclamation, the exegesis, of the invisible God (*exeghesato*, John 1.18: 'who has made him known'). Jesus, a human being in everything except sin (cf. Heb. 4.15), is the one in whom 'the whole fullness of deity dwells bodily' (Col. 2.9). Jesus is the icon, 'the image of the invisible God' (Col. 1.15). Indeed, in Jesus God meets man and man meets God. Truly, Jesus is the place of the Shekhinah, of God's Glory, and his humanity is the tent pitched by God in our midst.[12]

But there is more. The entire Fourth Gospel is shot through with the theme of the Glory that the Father confers on the Son, who manifests it to people through his words and acts. This glorification appears more clearly as Jesus draws nearer to death, at whose approach he exclaims: 'The hour has come for the Son of Man to be glorified' (John 12.23; cf. 13.31–32; 17.1–5). Jesus could see his death on the cross as glory because he had a reason for giving his life even to the point of death. He also had a reason for living: daily and gratuitous love for God and his brothers and sisters. This should be true not only for him but for all those who desire to follow him. 'Whoever serves me must follow me, and where I am, there will my servant be also' (John 12.26). This is why the risen Lord's last words in the Fourth Gospel, which he addressed to Peter, are particularly significant.

> 'When you were younger, you used to fasten your own belt and to go wherever you wished. But when you grow old, you will stretch out your hands, and someone else will fasten a belt around you and take you where you do not wish to go.' (He said this to indicate the kind of death by which he would glorify God.) After this he said to him, 'Follow me.'   (John 21.18–19)

Finally, it must not be forgotten that when Mary Magdalene goes to the tomb at dawn on Easter Day, she sees two angels in white garments, seated one at the head, the other at the feet, where Jesus' body had lain (John 20.12). This detail, which in all probability recalls the two Cherubim placed on the ark of the covenant, is intended to impress on the believer's heart a truth of the greatest importance: in the risen Jesus, the power of God's Shekhinah is active for ever.

In other words, after Jesus' earthly life, after his death and resurrection, the Temple is no longer the Lord's dwelling. The veil that at Jesus' death is rent from top to bottom (Mark 15.38 and parallels) prophetically attests to the end of the function of the holy of holies. The Temple, therefore, can soon vanish and, in effect, its end begins with Jesus' last words on the cross: 'It is finished' (John 19.30).[13] The meditation of the first Christians, encouraged first by the presence of the Temple in Jerusalem, then by its destruction by the Romans in AD 70, will understand this truth in depth and will end by affirming that Jesus is the new temple. 'He was speaking of the temple of his body. After he was raised from the dead, his disciples remembered that he had said this; and they believed the scripture and the word that Jesus had spoken' (John 2.21–22). His death meant the destruction of his body, but on the third day he was raised by God. The risen Jesus is the eschatological temple raised not by human hands (cf. Mark 14.58), but by God himself, to be 'a light for revelation to the Gentiles and for glory to your people Israel' (Luke 2.32). The risen Jesus is 'the greater and perfect tent (not made with hands)' (Heb. 9.11), which opened for us the way to the Father (cf. Heb. 10.20).[14] In the light of understanding Jesus as the new temple, God's dwelling in our midst, the Shekhinah seen by the disciples (cf. John 1.14; 1 John 1.1–4), it is clearer why Peter addressed him in these words: 'You are the Holy One of God; go away from me, Lord, for I am a sinful man!' (cf. Luke 5.8; John 6.69).

Now, if Jesus is the temple, the eschatological dwelling of God, Christians, who through faith, baptism and the Eucharist are incorporated into him to form one body, are also the temple of God. They are this both on the community level[15] and on the personal level. It is Paul who is the author of this revelation, all the more audacious if one recalls that he will address it to the Christians of Corinth when the Temple of stone was still standing in Jerusalem.[16]

> Do you not know that you are God's temple and that God's spirit dwells in you? . . . For God's temple is holy, and you are that temple. (1 Cor. 3.16–17)

> Do you not know that your body is a temple of the Holy Spirit within you, which you have from God, and that you are not your own? (1 Cor. 6.19)

Thanks to the indwelling of the Spirit in the depths of the heart, God becomes more present in us than we are to ourselves – *interior intimo meo*, according to Augustine's famous words in his *Confessions* III.6.11. As believers, we in our turn, discovering that we are the dwelling of God, dispose ourselves to 'glorify God in [our] body' (1 Cor. 6.20). Thus there is a passage from the ritual and sacral level of the Temple to the existential level of the person and his or her daily existence. Elsewhere, the same Paul, after declaring, 'We are the temple of the living God' (2 Cor. 6.16), immediately points out that this truth is the fulfilment of the promise made by God at the time of the exodus, a promise that runs like a leitmotiv through the whole of salvation history. 'I will place my dwelling in your midst . . . and I will walk among you, and will be your God, and you shall be my people' (Lev. 26.11–12; Ezek. 37.27). Again, however, it is John, more attentive than any other New Testament author to the theme of 'where is God?', who recalls some very important words of Jesus at the hour of his passage from this world to the Father (cf. John 13.1). 'Those who love me will keep my word, and my Father will love them, and we will come to them and make our home with them' (John 14.23). The Shekhinah of God the Father and Son, through the Holy Spirit, takes up his abode in the believer, in the Christian who loves Jesus and observes his word.[17] This is God's last dwelling in history. God's Glory was revealed on Mount Sinai; it descended to the tent of meeting in the midst of his people and journeyed with the children of Israel to the promised land; it followed the people into exile and returned with them to Jerusalem. Its place was the Temple, to which Jesus went, discerning the sacrament of God's Presence. Finally, the Shekhinah became a full and definitive Presence in Jesus Christ and through him, the Son of God who died and rose again, God the Three-in-One, dwells in every Christian.

Where is God? What is the place of his Presence? God takes up his dwelling in every Christian and, together, in the community of believers, the body of Christ, the temple of God.

> The definitive dwelling, the only Temple destined to replace all the provisional tabernacles, is the sanctuary that we are called to form, through Jesus, who lives in all of us and who with the Father and the Holy Spirit establishes God's dwelling among us.[18]

We can add that the eucharistic bread and wine, the body and blood of Jesus, are the sign of this Presence, the synthesis of all his life,[19] from his pre-existence with the Father until his coming in glory. His is a life spent in freedom and in love of God and humanity, teaching us to live as he lived and, when we die, to offer our lives promptly as he did, in the hope of entering eternal life together.

Conclusion

We cannot end our contemplative journey without turning our gaze to the end of history and of time, to the kingdom, as the seer of Revelation invites us to do. Awaiting and announcing the Lord's glorious coming, he writes:

> I saw the holy city, the new Jerusalem, coming down out of heaven from God, prepared as a bride adorned for her husband. And I heard a loud voice from the throne saying, 'See, the home of God is among mortals. He will dwell with them; they will be his peoples, and God himself will be with them.
> (Rev. 21.2–3; cf. Lev. 26.11–12; Ezek. 37.27; Isa. 7.14)

And, a little further: 'I saw no temple in the city, for its temple is the Lord God the Almighty and the Lamb' (Rev. 21.22).

Indeed, on the last day, this cosmos, this earth that we so love and to which we want to be fully faithful, will be transformed into 'a new heaven and a new earth' (Rev. 21.1). It will be the place where the kingdom is manifested, God's definitive dwelling in the midst of his people, now including all humankind. Then, finally, God will be all in all (1 Cor. 15.28), and we will be shown to be children of God, the body of Christ; we will be sons and daughters in the Son, becoming the Son, as Irenaeus of Lyons so splendidly says.

> For this, in fact, the Word became man and the Son of God became the Son of Man, so that man, joined with God and receiving adoption as a son, might become the son of God . . . The Word of God, our Lord Jesus Christ, on account of his great love (cf. Eph. 3.19), became what we are, to make us what he is.   (*Against Heresies* III.19.1; V, Preface)

Meanwhile, we continue to await in hope the final manifestation of God's Glory, invoking with words, and above all with our lives: 'Amen. Come, Lord Jesus!' (Rev. 22.20). We have the clear awareness that already today the Son, with the Father and the Spirit, makes his dwelling in us and makes of us his temple. This is now the dwelling place of the Shekhinah, the place in which the Father is to be adored in spirit and truth, that is, in the Holy Spirit and in Christ Jesus (cf. John 4.23–24). Therefore glorify God in your body (1 Cor. 6.20), in a community as well as a personal sense. In our bodies, we Christians are called to discern the Presence and to glorify it, by conducting ourselves honourably (cf. 1 Pet. 2.12) in a holy life, a life of love. Indeed, the God of Abraham, Jacob, Moses, Elijah and Isaiah, the God revealed to us in Jesus Christ, dwells in his community and in each one of us, if in faith and love we can recognize ourselves as his children and as brothers and sisters of one another, that is, if we can love one another as Jesus has loved us (cf. John 13.34; 15.12).

Notes

1 The faith of Abraham

1 Among the numerous works concerning the story of Abraham, I would like to mention: R. Martin-Achard, *Actualité d'Abraham*, Delachaux et Niestlé, Neuchâtel 1969; A. Segre, *Abramo nostro padre*, Carucci, Rome 1982; C. M. Martini, *Abramo nostro padre nella fede*, Borla, Rome 1983; *Abramo, padre di una moltitudine di uomini*, Biblia, Florence 1989; E. Moatti, P. Rocalve and M. Hamidullah, *Abraham*, Centurion, Paris 1992; T. Römer (ed.), *Abraham, nouvelle jeunesse d'un ancêtre*, Labor et Fides, Geneva 1997; V. Vogels, *Abraham: l'inizio della fede*, San Paolo, Cinisello Balsamo 1999; J. Cazeaux, *Le Partage de minuit: essai sur la Genèse*, Cerf, Paris 2006, pp. 199–417: C. Letta (ed.), *Abramo padre di tutti i credenti*, Ets, Pisa 2007.

2 The rabbinical tradition places great emphasis on the anti-idolatrous actions of Abraham, showing him on several occasions in the act of destroying the idols made by his father Terah; see L. Ginzberg, *Le leggende degli ebrei*, II, *Da Abramo a Giacobbe*, Adelphi, Milan 1997, pp. 23–6, 36–43, 230, 236–7.

3 These three moments of separation are dear to the monastic tradition that, starting from Gen. 12.1, has seen Abraham as a model of *xeniteia*, or the quality of an alien (see e.g. John Cassian, *Conferences* 3.6).

4 Here we find the origin of an idea that will be proclaimed by the prophets and will be brought to completion by Jesus: the driving power of faith erupts with great force and demands that the person called should abandon everything that could contradict, negate or impede the call of God. From such a call there arises the urgent need not to prefer anything to the love of God and the love of Christ.

5 Gregory of Nyssa, *Homilies on the Song of Songs* 8.

6 This person, also mentioned elsewhere in Scripture in Ps. 110.4 and Heb. 5.6, has even been included – by virtue of his offering of bread and wine – in the first Eucharistic Prayer, the so-called Roman Canon: 'Be pleased to look upon these offerings with a serene and kindly countenance, and to accept them, as once you were pleased

to accept . . . the sacrifice of Abraham, our father in faith, and the offering of your high priest Melchizedek, a holy sacrifice, a spotless victim.'

7 See the interesting comments of R. Fornara, *La visione contradetta: la dialettica fra visibilità e non-visibilità divina nella Bibbia ebraica*, Pontificio Instituto Biblico, Rome 2004, pp. 305–18.

8 A. Mello, 'Abramo, l'uomo del mattino', in *Parola, Spirito e Vita*, 36 (1997), p. 38.

2 Abraham and the binding of Isaac

1 See A. Segre, *Abramo nostro padre*, Carucci, Rome 1982, pp. 176–7.

2 See e.g. Augustine, *The City of God* XVI.32.1.

3 On the age of Isaac, see *Jerusalem Targum* on Gen. 22.1.

4 The author of the Second Book of Chronicles identifies the land of Moriah as the hill on which the temple of Jerusalem will be built (cf. 2 Chron. 3.1). Christian tradition from Origen onwards (*Commentary on Matthew* 126) has seen it as the hill where Jesus was crucified. cf. Caesarius of Arles, *Sermons* 84.5: 'The blessed presbyter Jerome wrote that he had learnt as a most reliable fact, from ancient and venerable authorities, that Christ the Lord was crucified in the place where Isaac had been offered in sacrifice . . . Moreover, certain ancient authorities assert that the first Adam was buried in the same place in which the cross was planted; and that place is called "the place of Calvary" because, according to tradition, the first member of the human race was buried there.'

5 It is interesting to note that Abraham had already referred to Isaac as 'the boy' in verse 5, when speaking to the two servants, as if, in their presence, he was already prepared to admit to the deed with which he was struggling in his own mind.

6 Origen, *Homilies on Genesis* 8.8.

7 C. M. Martini, *Abramo nostro padre nella fede*, Borla, Rome 1983, p. 122.

8 With regard to the rabbinical interpretations, a good synthesis may be found in L. Ginzberg, *Le leggende degli ebrei*, II, *Da Abramo a Giacobbe*, Adelphi, Milan 1997, pp. 93–103, 269–76; cf. also Segre, *Abramo nostro padre*, pp. 175–206. For the Church fathers, cf. M. Sheridan, *La Bibbia commentata dai padri: Antico Testamento*, I.2, Citta Nuova, Roma 2004, pp. 172–88. Modern and contemporary

commentaries: for a first bibliographical introduction, see A. Wénin, *Isacco o la prova di Abramo*, Cittadella, Assisi 2005, pp. 113–14; a good review of commentaries may be found in P. de Benedetti, 'Il sacrificio di Abramo in alcune grandi letture', in *Abramo, padre di una moltitudine di uomini*, Biblia, Florence 1989, pp. 105–64; see also F. Manns, *The Sacrifice of Isaac in the Three Monotheistic Religions*, Franciscan Printing Press, Jerusalem 1995.

9 *Genesis Rabbah* 56.8. The midrash suggests the possibility that *ha'alehu*, the verb used in verse 2 and usually translated 'offer him', may also be translated 'make him go up'. God would then have invited Abraham to take Isaac up the mountain with him, to offer a sacrifice with him.

10 Melitus of Sardis, *Fragments* 9.

11 John Chrysostom, *Homilies on John* 55.2.

12 *Midrash wa-yosha'* 1. I follow, with a few modifications, the translation of U. Neri, *Yl canto del mare*, Rome, Citta Nuova 1976, pp. 44–6, 51–5.

13 *Mekilta de-Rabbi Yishma'el* 8. See also 'Poema delle quattro notti' in *Targum Neofiti* on Exod. 12.42; the second night is that of the *'aqedah*.

14 E. Levinas, *Totalità e infinito*, Jaca Book, Milan 1990, p. 204.

15 John Chrysostom, *Homilies on Genesis* 47.3.

3 Jacob: the deceiver deceived, the victor vanquished

1 For an initial overview, see *Giacobbe, o l'avventura del figlio minore: atti del seminario invernale, Bocca di Magra, 9–12 febbraio 1989*, Biblia, Florence 1990; M. Sheridan, *La Bibbia commentata dai padri: Antico Testamento*, I.2, Citta Nuova, Roma 2004, pp. 225–335; J.-D. Macchi and T. Römer (ed.), *Jacob: commentaire à plusieurs voix de Genèse*, Labor et Fides, Geneva 2001, pp. 25–36; see J. Cazeaux, *Le Partage de minuit: essai sur la Genèse*, Cerf, Paris 2006, pp. 457–564.

2 As suggested by a note in the Jerusalem Bible.

3 Literally: 'in the place' with the definite article; but in the Jewish tradition 'the Place' (*ha-Maqom*) is one of the names of God.

4 The Hebrew text can also be translated: 'on him', that is, on Jacob. Jesus' affirmation: 'You will see heaven opened and the angels of God ascending and descending upon the Son of Man' (John 1.51) is understood in this way; most of the patristic commentaries on the episode of Jacob's ladder start from this Johannine text.

5 Or 'over him', Jacob. See *Genesis Rabbah* 69.2–3: 'The Lord stood over him, as the nurse stands over the infant's cradle to drive away the flies . . . He stood over him to protect him.'

6 In more modern language, we can say that dreams arise out of our experience and our desires; with Freud we can say that this is 'the royal road to the discovery of the unconscious'; but even after the work of psychoanalysis, dreams remain a mystery!

7 Irenaeus of Lyons, *Against Heresies* IV.14.1.

8 The Hebrew verb *abaq*, 'to fight', is related to a root that means 'to destroy'. We should note the subtle play of alliteration between the protagonist of the story, *Ya'aqov*, the place where the action happens, the bank of the *Yabboq* and the action of fighting, *abaq*.

9 I quote some of the rabbinical interpretations, collected and commented by E. Wiesel, *Personaggi biblici attraverso il midrash*, Cittadella, Assisi 1978, pp. 112–20.

10 According to the Talmud (*b. Chullin* 92a), it was the angel who wept and asked for mercy.

11 After Philo (see for example, *On the Change of Names* 81), the traditional interpretation of the name 'Israel' will be: 'the man who sees God' (*ish ra'ah El*).

4 Moses and the name of God

1 The bibliography on Moses is immense. For a first overview, see 'Moïse, l'homme de l'Alliance', in *Cahiers sioniens* 8 (1954); *L'umile grandezza di Mosè*, Biblia, Florence 1992. On the rabbinical tradition, see E. Fleg, *Mosè secondo i saggi*, Dehoniane, Naples 1981; for the Church fathers, see J. T. Lienhard (ed.), *La Bibbia commentata dai padri: Antico Testamento*, II, *Esodo, Levitico, Numeri, Deuteronomio*, Citta Nuova, Rome 2003. Finally, see A. Neher, *Mosè*, Mondadori, Milan 1961; M. Buber, *Mosè*, Marietti, Casale Monferrato 1983; A. Chouraqui, *Moïse*, Rocher, Monaco 1995.

2 Rashi of Troyes, *Commentary on Exodus* (Exod. 3.14).

3 Gregory of Nyssa, *Life of Moses* 2.232.

4 With great spiritual insight, the author of the Fourth Gospel puts the same questions on the lips of two disciples of Jesus, Thomas and Philip: 'How can we know the way?' (John 14.5); 'Lord, show us the Father' (John 14.8).

5 This could also be translated: 'I will be gracious as no one has ever been gracious.' In any case, this and the following 'will' are not meant in the sense of an arbitrary whim of God, but signify that *his love is born of freedom*, and depends neither on the force of necessity nor on chance circumstances.

6 It is worth remembering that, according to the hypothesis of the great Arab scholar Salomon D. Goitein, the meaning of these two passages could be even closer. According to Goitein, the root contained in the tetragram YHWH can denote a feeling of passion and intense love. Consequently, he proposes translating YHWH as 'He who acts with passion', 'The Passionate One'. Following his reasoning, the *Ehyeh asher ehyeh* of Exodus 3.14 could also be translated 'I am passionate towards the one who is passionate'. See A. Mello, 'Il Dio misericordioso e gli attribute della sua misericordia (Es 34,6–7)', in *Parola, Spirito e Vita*, 29 (1994), p. 40.

7 See P. Stefani, 'Mosè', in P. Stefani and G. Barbaglio, *Davanti a Dio*, EDB, Bologna 1995, p. 25: 'This passage of God before Moses, because of which only the "back" of God may be seen, marks the transition from the will to capture the glory of God by seeing it (this vision always leads back to oneself) to the readiness to listen (listening is the experience that leads us out of ourselves; one always listens to someone else).'

8 According to the Hebrew syntax, the subject of this and of the following 'proclaimed' could be either the Lord or Moses. I think that this is one of the cases in which the various meanings of Scripture may be seen in all their richness: it is not necessary to choose; either possibility is right.

9 Origen, *Homilies on Ezekiel* 6.6.

10 *Pirqe Avot* 2.16.

11 *Deuteronomy Rabbah* 7.11. See P. de Benedetti, *La morte di Mosè e altri esempi*, Bompiani, Milan 1971, pp. 9–11.

12 See for example *Jerusalem Targum* on Deut. 34.6; Philo, *On the Life of Moses* 2.291.

5 Elijah and the still small voice

1 Among the numerous works about Elijah, I would like to mention the fundamental *Élie le prophète*, I, *Selon les Écritures et les traditions*

chrétiennes, II, *Au Carmel, dans le Judaïsme et l'Islam*, Desclée de Brouwer, Paris 1956. See also C. M. Martini, *Il Dio vivente: riflessioni sul profeta Elia*, Piemme, Casale Monferrato 1990; E. Poirot, *Les prophètes Élie et Élisée dans la littérature chrétienne ancienne*, Brepols, Turnhout 1997; *Elia o il Mosè del silenzio*, Biblia, Florence 1999. 1 Kings 19, cf. J. Briend, 'Élie et l'expérience de Dieu', in J. Briend, *Dieu dans l'Écriture*, Cerf, Paris 1992, pp. 13–39; B. Carucci Viterbi, 'L'esperienza di Dio sull'Oreb di Elia', in *Parola, Spirito e Vita*, 30 (1994), pp. 49–60; A. Mello, 'Una voce silenziosa: l'esperienza spirituale di Elia', in *Parola, Spirito e Vita*, 38 (1998), pp. 19–28.

2 See E. Poirot, *Élie, archétype du moine*, Abbaye de Bellefontaine, Begrolles-en-Mauges 1995.

3 Martini, *Il Dio vivente*, p. 83.

4 It is known that the name Horeb is given to Sinai in the so-called 'Deuteronomic' tradition, to which the first book of Kings also belongs.

5 See M. Masson, *Elia, l'appello del silenzio*, EDB, Bologna 1993, pp. 25–9.

6 See *b. Megillah* 19b.

7 *Midrash Tanhuma, Pequdé* 3.

8 In the Bible, the word *demamà* is found elswhere only in Job 4.16 and Psalm 107.29, both with the meaning of 'silence'. Among the numerous translations of the expression *qol demamà daqqà* are: 'a voice, a gentle silence' (A. Chouraqui), 'the murmur of a silence that fades away' (M. Buber) and 'the rustle of a faint murmur' (TOB Bible, Traduction Oecuménique de la Bible). The choice of 'the murmur of a light breeze' in the CEI Bible (Conferenza Episcopale Italiana) is inspired by the Vulgate *sibilus aurae tenuis* (cf. LXX: *phone auras leptes*).

9 L. Mazzinghi, 'Elia e la voce del silenzio', in *Parole di Vita*, 46.5 (2001), p. 17.

10 Gregory the Great, *Moral Commentary on Job* V.66.

11 *Songs of the Sabbath Sacrifice* fr. 20.II.7–8, 12–14.

6 The vocation of Isaiah

1 *The Ascension of Isaiah* 3.6–10.

2 See *Ascension* 5.1, 11–14; *Lives of the Prophets* 1.

3 Among the numerous studies of this text, I would like to mention: J. Steinmann, 'La vocation prophétique d'Isaïe', in *Cahiers sioniens*,

3 (1949), pp. 130–43; R. Knierim, 'The Vocation of Isaiah', in *Vetus Testamentum*, 18 (1968), pp. 47–68; J. Vermeylen, *Du prophète Isaïe à l'apocalyptique*, I, Gabalda, Paris 1977, pp. 187–97; A. Mello, *Isaia: commento esegetico-spirituale*, Qiqajon, Bose 1986, pp. 22–8; O. Kaiser, *Isaia: capitoli 1–12*, Paideia, Brescia 1998, pp. 159–80; B. Marconcini, 'Il racconto della vocazione (Is 6,1–13)', in B. Marconcini (ed.), *Logos: corso di studi biblici*, III, *Profeti e apocalittici*, 2nd edn, Elle Di Ci, Leumann 2007, pp. 275–88.

4 Cf. B. Renaud, 'La vocation d'Isaïe expérience de la foi', in *La Vie spirituelle*, 119 (1968), pp. 129–45.

5 Cf. M. Buber, *La fede dei profeti*, Marietti, Casale Monferrato 1985, pp. 125–33.

6 The title *YHWH zeva'ot* means literally 'Lord of hosts, of armies'. Such a name originally described the Lord as the commander of earthly armies (cf. 1 Sam. 17.45); after the opposition of the prophets to the pagan cults of the stars, this name came to describe God as the Lord of the cosmic armies, of all the creatures of earth and heaven (cf. Amos 5.8), hence 'Lord of the universe'. This last is the meaning of this title in the present passage.

7 See *Segno di unità: le più antiche eucaristie della chiesa*, ed. by the brothers and sisters of Bose and E. Mazza, Qiqajon, Bose 1996, pp. 153–6.

8 For a detailed historical analysis, see R. Taft, *Il Sanctus nell'anfora: un riesame della questione*, Orientalia Christiana, Rome 1999; see also N. Moro, 'Cantare con gli angeli: *Sanctus/Qedushà* nella tradizione giudaica e cristiana', in *Qol*, 32/33 (1991), pp. 5–7.

9 The verb *nidmeti* may also be rendered 'struck dumb', a suggestive translation in the light of the Seraphim's gesture of touching the lips of the prophet.

10 See P. Sacchi, 'Isaia 6 e la concezione di impurità nel medio giudaismo', in *Vivens homo*, 13.1 (2002), pp. 55–77; see P. Sacchi, *Sacro/profano impuro/puro nella Bibbia e dintorni*, Morcelliana, Brescia 2007.

11 See C. A. Evans, *To See and Not Perceive: Isaiah 6,9–10 in Early Jewish and Christian Interpretation*, JSOT Press, Sheffield 1989; J.-P. Sonnet, 'Le motif de l'endurcissement (Is 6,9–10) et la lecture d'"Isaïe"', in *Biblica*, 73 (1992), pp. 208–39.

7 Where is God?

1 Here I echo the title of a splendid book of biblical theology: S. Terrien, *The Elusive Presence: The Heart of Biblical Theology*, Harper and Row, San Francisco 1978.

2 L. Bouyer, *Gnosis: la conoscenza di Dio nella Scrittura*, Libreria Editrice Vaticana, Rome 1991, p. 38.

3 For a fuller treatment of this text, see E. Bianchi, *Adamo, dove sei?*, Qiqajon, Bose 1994, pp. 89–151.

4 See N. Negretti, *The Seventh Day*, Biblical Institute Press, Rome 1973, pp. 164 and 251: 'As at the end of the creation of the universe there is the divine rest (Gen. 2.2–3), so at the end of the construction of the tabernacle there is the descent of the divine Glory (Exod. 40.34) . . . The final meaning of the seventh day and the supreme demands of the covenant unite in announcing and communicating the definitive agreement of God with humankind, which is his *shakan* in the midst of Israel.' On the seventh day, see also A. J. Heschel's classic work, *The Sabbath: Its Meaning for Modern Man*, Rusconi, Milan 1972.

5 The image of the Cloud expresses once more the impossibility for human beings to see the Glory of God fully on this earth. With reference to this, see the dialogue between God and Moses (Exod. 33.20, 22–23), with commentary above.

6 For a significant Jewish point of view on the subject of the Glory of God, see A. J. Heschel, *God in Search of Man*, Borla, Turin 1969, pp. 98–105.

7 Cf. E. E. Urbach, *Les Sages d'Israël*, Cerf, Paris 1996, pp. 43–72 and 721–9.

8 Even more precisely, the Presence of God was recognized in the empty space between the two Cherubim placed over the ark of the covenant, situated in the holy of holies (cf. Exod. 25.1–22; Num. 7.89; 1 Kings 8.6–7 etc.: God is 'enthroned on the cherubim' (1 Sam. 4.4; 2 Sam. 6.2; Ps. 99.1; cf. 2 Kings 19.15).

9 The Virgin of Nazareth is the ark of the covenant – as the profound spiritual insight of the Church has understood, defining her as *foederis arca* – and, as such, she spreads joy and blessings around her (cf. Luke 1.41–45; 2 Sam. 6.11–15).

10 M. Buber, *Tales of the Chasidim*, Guanda, Parma 1992, p. 57.

11 See P. Lenhardt, 'La Tradition d'Israël sur la Présence Divine (Shekinah) dans le Temple et dans le monde éclaire la foi chrétienne en l'Incarnation', in *Cahiers Ratisbonne*, 2 (1997), pp. 137–62.

12 Cf. Terrien, *Elusive Presence*, p. 420: 'This is the stumbling block of the Gospel: the eternal divinity has become a human being in time.'

13 Isaac of Nineveh has left us a suggestive reflection on the link between the Shekhinah and the cross: 'The Shekhinah which shines from the ark has mysteriously taken up its abode on the cross. The power of the Shekhinah is fully manifested on the cross' (*Second Part* XI.5–6). He understood that on the cross the true glory of Jesus Christ was manifested, the glory of one who has loved unto the end (cf. John 13.1).

14 Cf. A. Vanhoye, 'Sanctuaire terrestre, sanctuaire céleste dans l'Épître aux Hébreux', in C. Focant (ed.), *Quelle maison pour Dieu?*, Cerf, Paris 2003, pp. 351–94.

15 On this subject see also Eph. 2.21 and 1 Pet. 2.4–5.

16 See E. Bianchi, 'Non sapete che lo Spirito di Dio abita in voi?', Qiqajon, Bose 1998.

17 On the theme of the indwelling of God in the believer, see also N. Siffe-Wiederhold, *La Présence divine à l'individu d'après le Nouveau Testament*, Cerf, Paris 2005.

18 L. Bouyer, 'La *Shekinah*: Dieu avec nous', in *Bible et vie chrétienne*, 20 (1957–8), p. 22.

19 See Irenaeus of Lyons, *Against Heresies* III.16.7.